Navigating the Journey

Navigating the Journey: Advocating for your Gifted Child

Gemma Permanand

GVP Publishing

The advice and strategies found within may not be suitable for every situation. This work is sold with the understanding that neither the author nor the publisher are held responsible for the results accrued from the advice in this book. While every caution has been taken to provide the most accurate information, the author makes no representations or warranties as to accuracy, completeness, suitability or validity of any information in this book and is not liable for any errors, omissions or delays in this information or any losses, injurues or damages arising from its display or use. The publisher cannot accpet responsibility for facts that become outdated or for inadvertant errors or omissions.

Copyright © 2021 Gemma Permanand

All rights reserved. No part of this publication may be reproduced, distributed, or transmitted in any form or by any means, including photocopying, recording, or other electronic or mechanical methods, without the prior written permission of the publisher, except in the case of brief quotations embodied in critical reviews and certain other noncommercial uses permitted by copyright law.

Gemma Permanand has no responsibility for the persistence or accuracy of URLs for external or third-party Internet Websites referred to in this publication and does not guarantee that any content on such Websites is, or will remain, accurate or appropriate.

Cover Design by Andy Meaden

First Printing July 2021

ISBN 978-0-9963541-1-0

Navigating the Journey
gemma@ntjguide.com

Acknowledgements

It has been a whirlwind since finding out my child was gifted and a long and difficult road in many respects. We are lucky to have had a great deal of support from educational consultants, our school, GiftedWA and Mensa Australia so thank you to all those people who have given us support and advice.

Thanks also to all those who gave feedback and advice on the content of this book – your time and insight has been invaluable and has helped to make this book a stronger resource.

Lastly, thank you to all the other parents out there advocating and trying to get the best possible scenario for their children. Raising a gifted child is a challenge and by advocating for our children, hopefully we can raise awareness of giftedness and make some of our challenges a little easier!

"All of us do not have equal talent, but all of us should have an equal opportunity to develop our talent."

John F. Kennedy

Contents

Introduction 1

1. What Exactly is Gifted Anyway? 3

2. A Suspected Giftie – Now What? 13

3. Understanding IQ Tests – What Are They Really Testing? 21

4. Results – What Do They Really Mean? 51

5. So Where Do We Go From Here? 61

6. The Big Question – Schooling! 70

7. Putting it into Practice – Getting the Best Fit for your Child 88

8. The Twice-Exceptional Child 108

9. The Gifted Personality 118

Conclusion 145

Glossary *148*

Resources *152*

Index *172*

Introduction

"So, your child is gifted." You may have heard these words from a psychologist or perhaps you strongly suspect you have a gifted child. One of the first reactions people may have is to congratulate you and your child. But you may not feel the same way or understand what that means for your family – and that's ok! Navigating life with a gifted child is uncertain and, at times, challenging, but this book is here to guide you through the first steps on the journey.

There are probably many reasons that prompted you to pick up this book and for some of you, this will be the beginning of your journey. Others will already be a little way down the road but still looking for advice and direction. Wherever you are on your journey with your child, this book can help offer some insight. It is important to note though that this isn't an educational textbook or a psychological guide. It is a parent's guide, written by a parent of a gifted child for others who are struggling or just want the benefit of communicating with someone who is also going through those same things.

When my child was first identified as gifted, I felt overwhelmed and somewhat alone. I was desperate to

INTRODUCTION

understand what this all meant and whether this changes things for my child, and me, as the parent of a gifted child. There are many support groups and networks out there, but until you find and tap into them, it can be a very isolating experience. The goal of this book is to be your companion through those first days, weeks, even years; to share hints and tips as well as a discussion of some of the research surrounding giftedness. I will also discuss schooling and potential pitfalls and options there.

The book has been designed in such a way as to take you on a journey from initial impressions of giftedness to testing and ultimately to a happy child. However, not all journeys will be the same and not all of you will be picking up this book at the same point in your stories. So, each chapter is also designed to be read independently. If you have already gone through testing and are looking to learn more about schooling options, then dive straight into the school chapter. There are links to research and resources at the back of the book, arranged by chapter as well as a list of general resources and an explanation of the terms and abbreviations used in the book.

Gifted children are very complex, amazing, talented and exceptional individuals. Raising a gifted child is exhausting, exhilarating, frustrating, and amazing, often in equal measures. But by trying to understand a bit more about the challenges involved and what to look for, you can hopefully be the best advocate for your child and raise a happy, well-adjusted child.

1

What Exactly is Gifted Anyway?

One of the first and most important things to sort out is to make sure that we are all on the same page when we talk about gifted children. So, the fundamental question is, what is a gifted child?

It is harder than you might think to answer that question definitively. For many people, they see giftedness as synonymous with academic ability. However, many experts in giftedness would disagree, although it is important to note that there is no one clear definition of giftedness. Generally, though, giftedness is distinct from academic ability in so far as giftedness is the cognitive potential to achieve whereas academic ability is a concrete achievement. Contrary to popular belief, not all gifted children achieve well academically. Partly this can be down to a lack of understanding of how they learn, but it can also be down to the personality of the gifted child. One of the key parenting challenges with gifted children is to gain the understanding of your child's specific needs in order to help them fulfil their cognitive potential.

What is cognitive potential and how is it different from academic achievement?

Cognitive skills are essentially the mechanism of how we learn and refer to the brain's ability to process and filter information which is needed for acquiring knowledge and for reasoning, among other things. Cognitive potential assesses the brain's ability to acquire these skills.

A person may test highly in an IQ test – which tests cognitive potential – and this means that they have the right building blocks to learn. Academic achievement on the other hand, is the use of these cognitive skills to master concepts such as reading, writing and mathematics. Just because a child has the cognitive potential, it does not mean academic achievement will always follow as there are many factors which influence this, some of which are discussed in this book.

In 1991, The Columbus Group coined this definition of giftedness, which is a great place to start in trying to gain an understanding of what giftedness actually is: "Giftedness is asynchronous development in which advanced cognitive abilities and heightened intensity combine to create inner experiences and awareness that are qualitatively different from the norm. This asynchrony increases with higher intellectual capacity. The uniqueness of the gifted renders them particularly vulnerable and requires modifications in parenting, teaching and counselling in order for them to develop optimally."

Now, let's look at that definition in a bit more detail. At first it can, like so many other things on this journey, seem a bit overwhelming. Essentially it implies you need to parent in a different way – but how? Why?

Who are the Columbus Group?

The Columbus Group is a group established in the late 1980s in Columbus, Ohio. It was composed of parents, educators and psychologists who sought to challenge the view gaining ground in the 1980s that giftedness was synonymous with achievement. Their experience with gifted children led them to question this view as they saw giftedness appearing early in life in many children and often with other unusual traits. This led them to adopt the definition which looked at asynchronous development.

One of the key things that helped me to really understand giftedness, and also which made me a stronger advocate for my child, was understanding that there are fundamental physical differences in the way a gifted person's brain functions compared to a neurotypical brain.

A majority of the research into giftedness has been in the field of psychology; however, there have been a few neurological studies carried out more recently. Examining the brains of gifted people with MRI and MEG technology has shown scientists that gifted brains are different. The brain of a gifted person has more grey matter, that is, the brain matter that is physically used to compute information. Gifted brains also show stronger neural connections – these are the pathways in our brains that move information. So, a gifted child is able to recall/compute/interpret information faster than neurotypical peers due to the increased grey matter and make connections faster due to the stronger neural connections. This fundamental physical difference makes it clear that there is a distinct group of gifted people, and, perhaps more importantly, they are different from those who have neurotypical brains but high academic ability.

What is Grey Matter?

Grey matter refers to a type of brain tissue within the central nervous system which processes information. It comprises around 40% of all brain tissue.

White matter refers to a type of brain tissue within the central nervous system which transports information around the central nervous system. It comprises around 60% of all brain tissue.

Now that we understand that research has shown that gifted brains are distinct in particular ways from neurotypical brains, it goes some way to explaining why we need to make a specific distinction between giftedness and high academic ability or talent.

To further explain and understand this distinction, it is useful to look at Gagné's Differentiated Model of Giftedness and Talent. Dr Françoys Gagné is a French-Canadian psychologist who devoted a great part of his career to the study of gifted and talented individuals. He won several awards for his work in the field, including two awards from

American Mensa in 1993 and 1998 and a distinguished scholar award from the National Association for Gifted Children in 1996. In a move away from literature proposing that giftedness was synonymous with achievement, Gagné proposed a model which differentiated between giftedness and talent. He identified four ability domains:

- intellectual ability – e.g. reasoning, memory, judgement
- creative abilities – e.g. inventiveness, imagination, originality
- socioaffective ability – e.g. perceptiveness, communication, influence
- sensorimotor abilities – e.g. strength, endurance, coordination

To Gagné, the term giftedness designates the possession and use of untrained and spontaneously expressed natural abilities (called aptitudes or gifts), in at least one of his four identified ability domains, to a degree that places an individual in at least the top 10% of his or her age peers. By contrast, the term talent designates the superior mastery of systematically developed abilities (or skills) and knowledge in at least one field of human activity to a degree that places a child's achievement within the upper 10% of age peers who are active in that field or fields.

Gagné's model proposes a clear difference between gifted and talented. Gifted children can also be talented, but they are not synonymous. Equally, talented children may also be gifted but this is not always the case. As Gagné describes it, giftedness is a natural ability that places them above 90% of the population. But these differences do not always lead to talent and success. Indeed, a gifted child may well underachieve and be falling behind age peers in many ways. So why would that be the case? The cognitive potential of gifted individuals suggests they have the potential to far outstrip the expectations of their age range so why would they not be fulfilling this?

It is interesting to pause and examine another well-renowned definition of giftedness. Joseph Renzulli is an American educational psychologist, affiliated to the National Research Center on the Gifted and Talented, located at the University of Connecticut. He has also served on the White House task force on Education of the Gifted and Talented and has won the so-called "Nobel Prize for Education", the Harold W. McGraw Jr. Award for Innovation in Education.

Renzulli proposed a Three Ring Concept of Giftedness. Simply put, the Three Ring Concept proposes that there are three critical factors which are responsible for the development of gifted behaviour:

1. above average ability
2. creativity – defined as fluency, flexibility, originality of thought, openness to experience, sensitivity to stimulus and willingness to take risks
3. task commitment – defined as perseverance, endurance, hard work, self-confidence, perceptiveness, and a special fascination for the subject

Renzulli makes a further distinction within above average ability between general ability, such as processing information and abstract thinking, and specific abilities such as the capacity to acquire information or to perform an activity. To Renzulli an individual needs to demonstrate above average ability in one or more areas – this could be a specific area like musical talent or mathematical ability or it could be a more general group of abilities.

In order for gifted behaviour to be displayed, all three factors need to be present. The key concept within this model is that Renzulli argues that high potential individuals may only turn this potential into talent if their environment encourages it; without an encouraging environment, you will struggle to get all three factors. So this model gives an insight into why it is possible that a gifted individual may underachieve.

Asynchronous development

In discussions on giftedness and gifted children, the words *asynchronous development* are used often. This is because children, even gifted children, develop at different rates and are individuals. A gifted child does not have to be gifted across the board – as Renzulli and Gagné state, there are different types of above average abilities and a gifted child may be gifted in many areas or in just one or two. This is perfectly normal, but it can pose a challenge when trying to find a workable education solution, especially if the child is years ahead of age peers in one area but working on the same level as them in other subjects. (More on schooling and finding the right fit in chapters 6 and 7).

Can we define gifted?

We have now looked at and discussed a few definitions of giftedness as well as looking at some of the physical differences present and some of the difficulties in identification so can we now put some clarity around what a gifted child is?

Let's recap what we know:

A gifted child:

- has high cognitive potential
- often shows asynchronous development
- has natural aptitudes or abilities which haven't been taught that place them in the top 10% of their age group
- has a brain that has physical differences to a neurotypical brain
- does not always show gifted behaviours in all circumstances
- may not always perform or achieve well academically

These are all abstract concepts and it does become difficult to make them more concrete in any meaningful way in a book such as this. That is because, like all people, gifted children are individuals and their giftedness may manifest in many different ways. Just because your child doesn't show a particular trait, it does not mean they are not gifted – they may still be and their particular strand of giftedness may just look completely atypical. So, whilst we now get into a discussion of what sort of behaviours may be an indication of giftedness, please keep in mind that this is by no means an exhaustive list.

Often when we hear *gifted* we think about child prodigies who finish university at 10 or who are amazing concert pianists at a very young age. It is true that these children show amazing talents and abilities but it does not mean that all children need to follow this path in order to be gifted.

However, there are a few traits which are generally found to be more common among gifted children and the presence of these traits could well indicate a gifted child. According to the National Association for Gifted Children these include:

- unusual alertness (including from infancy)
- quick learner – able to pick up new concepts at a rapid rate
- excellent memory – ability to retain and recall information
- an unusually large vocabulary and complex sentence structure compared to other children of a similar age
- an advanced understanding of abstract ideas and concepts such as word nuance and metaphors
- an enjoyment of problem solving – for example with numbers or puzzles
- intellectual curiosity – constant questions and persistently seeking more knowledge
- high levels of energy – needing very little down-time

Studies of gifted children find that they often learn to read much earlier than age peers and can also grasp concepts such as telling time at a young age. Often these abilities will be self-taught and a parent will just notice that their child seems suddenly able to read or tell time or do complex mathematics in comparison to normal expectations for their age. This links back to Gagné's definition of untrained and spontaneous abilities.

Whilst early reading and a large complex vocabulary are very often synonymous with giftedness, the lack of these traits does not exclude giftedness as a definition. Albert Einstein, for example, was a late talker who did not learn to read until he was 7. Children, even gifted children, develop at different rates and as we know from examining the definition of giftedness, asynchronous development is a part of giftedness.

So, it may be that your child can draw perfect anatomically correct portraits from an early age but cannot read. Likewise, a child reading chapter books by the time they are 3 may not be able to draw an identifiable flower or take turns in the playground. This is perfectly normal. Remember, at the end of the day, gifted children are still children!

2

A Suspected Giftie – Now What?

Perhaps you have read the previous chapter and are thinking that a lot of the information sounds familiar or perhaps you picked up this book because you strongly suspect your child is gifted. But what do you do now?

Well, the answer is it depends! There are a few avenues open to you and the right one will depend on your current needs and circumstances. For example, do you have a decision point coming up – a house move or school move; is your child happy or unhappy at school?

All these things will need to be taken into account. It may also be that what works now, will not in the future and you may return here to assess other potential options.

Do nothing

Yes, this is a perfectly valid option! If your child is happy and thriving, then doing nothing is absolutely a choice and may be the right call. Just continue to be observant as things can change quickly as a child grows and progresses through school. If you do run into problems further down the line, always remember that you suspect your child is gifted and consider ruling that in or out as a factor that could be causing issues.

Support and encourage

You could choose to support and encourage what you perceive as your child's natural abilities whilst also watching for signs of asynchronous development and supporting any areas that need additional help. This can all be done without any formal diagnosis of giftedness provided you have the resources and support to do this. If your child has not yet started school, you can develop activities to nurture their abilities at home. If they are at school, then you are likely to need the help of the school and the class teacher in supporting and encouraging your child. As long as the school is open and happy to this and your child is happy and thriving then no formal testing may be necessary. But do keep in mind that your child may change or they may have a different relationship with a teacher in a subsequent year and what had been working before may not any more.

Formal IQ testing

The only definitive way to find out if your child is gifted is to have them take a formal IQ test. This will give you a report which you can then use in the future when advocating for your child. Formal IQ testing is the only real way to provide an actual quantifiable answer to the question of whether an individual is gifted, but it may not be the solution for everyone. IQ testing is expensive and there are considered to be optimum ages for IQ testing which you may decide to wait for.

IQ tests can also highlight areas of potential weakness in a gifted child so can be useful in identifying other possible areas which need to be considered (more on this in chapter 8). We know from our discussion of the definition of giftedness that asynchronous development is common, but weaknesses can often be overlooked if the child is excelling in many other areas and this oversight can cause problems later on. IQ tests also allow for formal identification of giftedness; having this certainty as early as possible can help ensure that your child has the right tools necessary to convert their natural abilities into talent.

How do I decide what to do?

There are many factors to consider in deciding which way to progress once you suspect a gifted child and there is no right answer. The decision you make is personal to your family and your current set of circumstances. But here are a few things to weigh up when trying to make the decision:

- Is my child currently happy and thriving in home and school?
- Does my child have a supportive teacher at school?
- Is there a decision point coming up? A move, new school, access to gifted and talented programmes, scholarships, etc.

- Would we change anything if we had a formal IQ test?
- Is my child a good age to be formally tested?

If you decide to go down the route of formal IQ testing, then there are more decisions to be made as several different tests are accepted and used depending on where you are located, the age of the child and the person administering the test. The following chapter discusses a few of the main tests available in more detail and also some of the pros and cons of each.

But I'm not sure...is my child really gifted?

This is a common feeling – I know it was one I had many times! The best way it was explained to me is that you, as parents, have grown up with your child; to you what they do and how they act is normal but when outsiders observe the child, they see things that are not normal compared to age peers.

There is also a strong likelihood that giftedness is an inherited trait – indeed a survey of behavioural and social educators and scientists by Snyderman and Rothman in 1987 showed that of the over 1000 surveyed, most believed that heredity played an important role in IQ scores. What this means is that there is a strong possibility that one or other of the parents and possibly some of the extended family may also be gifted to some degree. This can make it more difficult for parents to see giftedness in their children as the characteristics they display can often be more common within the family and therefore less likely to draw attention.

These factors mean it is relatively common for families not to be aware that their child is gifted until it is pointed out to them by an outsider. Unfortunately, this may also be missed at school simply because giftedness presents in different ways and the concept of giftedness is not one that much, if any, time is spent on in standard teacher training. For these reasons, it is possible that both the parents and the teacher may be surprised by a suggestion of giftedness. Often in these cases, the suggestion may come from a trained professional.

But it doesn't so much matter how or even when you came to the realisation that your child is gifted. Everyone has their own personal journey and the manifestations of giftedness are so disparate that it can be hard to see. What matters most is that now that you know, you have the information you need to help your child thrive in the best possible way.

IQ testing

So, you suspect or have had it brought to your attention that your child may be gifted. You have thought about it and come to the decision that you want to get a formal IQ test done. But how do you go about it?

Firstly, it is important that you really understand what an IQ test is: it is a test of cognitive ability not achievement. Schools sometimes give group IQ tests but these are not overly useful in determining giftedness as they tend to be more inaccurate at higher levels of IQ as they are standardised questions which are not adjusted based on performance. If you are specifically looking for an IQ test to rule in or out the possibility of giftedness then an individual test is far superior.

These tests should only be administered by a professional – usually an educational psychologist. If possible, try to find one who has experience working with gifted children. If your child develops a good rapport with the tester and they are familiar with gifted children, then your chance of an accurate result is increased. For example, gifted children often switch off and disengage when a task is too easy; if the tester is not experienced with gifted children and starts from the easiest questions for that age range, asking until a mistake or set number of incorrect answers is made then the child may disengage from the test process and the result will be under-representative of true IQ. By choosing an individual who has experience in these situations, they may mitigate this scenario by, for example, starting the questions at a higher level therefore reducing the likelihood of fatigue or disengagement.

It is also important to consider the age of the child when testing. It is possible to have an IQ test administered from the age of 2 but, generally, it is believed that the optimal time to test is around 6 years old. It is possible to obtain an accurate result if testing children younger than this but several other factors come into play.

In young children, their ability to concentrate is often not as developed and therefore they can get tired and switch off during testing, leading to a lower than expected score. In cases like this, when a child is re-tested at an older age, their score often dramatically improves.

Secondly, some of the tests designed for younger children have lower ceilings so if a child is in the upper age range for that particular test, they may hit the ceiling before reaching their full potential, therefore underestimating their IQ.

There are many different IQ tests available, but in this book we will concentrate on four of the most commonly used tests when assessing IQ in gifted children:

- Stanford-Binet
- Woodcock Johnson
- Weschler Intelligence Scale for Children
- Weschler Preschool and Primary Scale of Intelligence

We will look at each of these in turn and examine their pros and cons in the following chapter. But first let's look at the general structure of these tests.

Generally speaking, IQ tests are composed of a series of subtests, each of which will be designed to test a certain area of cognitive ability (such as verbal comprehension, working memory, fluid reasoning, etc.). Each subtest will be marked out of a certain number; if the maximum score is obtained on a subtest then the candidate has achieved a ceiling score in that area. The scores from these subtests are then aggregated using the test prescribed formula and a full scale IQ (FSIQ) number is derived.

IQ tests work on a bell curve with a series of standard deviations. When the tests are designed, the scores are normed so the average of the results is set to an IQ of 100 – which is deemed to be an average IQ score. Most tests then use standard deviations of either 15 or 16 IQ points. Whenever the tests are revised, they are once again normed to 100.

A phenomenon known as the Flynn Effect has shown that IQ within the population can increase over time, which is why re-norming the test to 100 in every revision is so important. So when test takers take older versions of the tests, they usually score higher than if they were to take the current version of the test. For this reason, it is important to ensure that your child takes the most current version of the test available in order to produce the most accurate result.

The Flynn Effect

The Flynn Effect is a phenomenon named after James Flynn, a researcher and lecturer who researched the change in IQ scores through subsequent generations. The Flynn Effect refers to the suggestion that IQ increases within a population over time and therefore you will naturally see a rise in test scores of around 0.25–0.3 IQ points per year since the test was normed. It has been suggested that this can be attributed to longer years of schooling, better nutrition and increased access to information through new technology.

However, it has also been shown that the Flynn Effect is most noticeable at lower IQ scores and the increase has been said to be negligible at higher scores. There is also research by Flynn and others showing that the Flynn Effect may be reversing with subsequent generations of test takers in countries such as Norway, UK and Australia showing lower IQ scores over a period of time.

3

Understanding IQ Tests – What Are They Really Testing?

This chapter looks in detail at four of the more commonly used IQ tests in the following order:

- Stanford-Binet
- Weschler Intelligence Scale for Children
- Weschler Preschool and Primary Scale of Intelligence
- Woodcock Johnson Test of Cognitive Abilities

There are a few things to consider when choosing which test is right for your child. Although all the tests will give a formal IQ score, there are a few differences in the tests themselves and additional scores which can be calculated.

By understanding the pros and cons of each test, you can hopefully make an informed decision. Other points to consider when choosing a test are discussed in further detail at the end of the chapter.

Stanford-Binet

History of the test

The Stanford-Binet test is perhaps the oldest intelligence test in the world. Alfred Binet was a French psychologist who created the first IQ test that had wide usage. Binet was commissioned by the French government to create an intelligence scale that would identify children needing additional help in schools. He teamed up with Theodore Simon to create a series of tests that focused on mental abilities such as memory rather than on academic or learned abilities as had been the focus of previous tests. This intelligence scale came to be known as the Simon-Binet Intelligence Scale and was in use from around 1905.

Lewis Terman, a psychologist at Stanford University, updated and adapted the test in 1916 and this American adaptation became known as the Stanford-Binet test. It is an updated version of this format of the test that is in use today.

Current version

The current version of the Stanford-Binet is the SB-V which was updated in 2003.

The Stanford-Binet test is currently on its fifth revision. Since its creation in 1916, it has been updated in 1937, 1960, 1973, 1986 and 2003.

The current version takes around 45–90 minutes to complete depending on the pace, age and concentration of the test taker.

Age range

The Stanford-Binet test can currently be sat by children from the age of 2, all the way to adults and has been normed for ages 2 to 85. The test is differentiated through the means of different question sets for different age groups.

Score classification

The current version of the Stanford-Binet test uses a different classification of scores than the previous version. The current classifications are shown in the table below. The SB-V uses a standard deviation of 15.

IQ Range	IQ Classification
145-160	Very gifted or highly advanced
130-144	Gifted or very advanced
120-129	Superior
110-119	High average
90-109	Average
80-89	Low average
70-79	Borderline impaired or delayed
55-69	Mildly impaired or delayed
40-54	Moderately impaired or delayed

Subtests

The SB-V currently has five subtests, but each subtest has a verbal and a non-verbal component so it is possible to get ten subtest scores. The introduction of the non-verbal test for every subtest is new to the fifth edition of the test and allows for the testing of young children and people with language difficulties as equal weight is given to non-verbal as verbal subtests. In addition to scores for the subtests, a full scale IQ (FSIQ), a non-verbal IQ and a verbal IQ are also generated.

The subtests in the SB-V are:

- Fluid Reasoning – this measures the ability to solve problems using inductive or deductive reasoning and problem solving without advance preparation. The verbal subtest uses picture problems and verbal absurdities and asks the test taker to explain the solution or absurdity. The non-verbal subtest uses objects and matrices to solve patterns and spatial problems.

- Knowledge – this measures the general acquired information of the test taker. It evaluates their understanding of their surroundings and their ability to recall information from long-term memory. The non-verbal subtest uses visual absurdities and gestures whilst the verbal subtest asks for explanations of objects or words.

- Quantitative Reasoning – this measures the ability to work with and manipulate numbers and numerical reasoning. The non-verbal subtest uses tools such as number tapping whilst the verbal subtest looks at things such as geometric problems and estimation.

- Visual/Spatial Reasoning – this measures the ability to see patterns, relationships and spatial orientations of visual displays. The non-verbal subtest uses foam pattern pieces and boards to create a display and the verbal subtest asks for explanations of direction and spatial observation based on diagrams and pictures.
- Working Memory – this measures the ability to recall facts and information from short-term memory. The non-verbal subtest uses things such as recalling where an object has been hidden and tapping out a sequence. The verbal subtest asks for the recall of last words or items from a previously elaborated sentence.

Ceiling scores

The SB-V has a FSIQ ceiling of 160 and each subtest has a ceiling score of 19. What this means is that if your child hits the ceiling on the test or subtests, they could not have scored any higher on that particular test or section regardless of how many more questions they answered. In cases where the ceiling scores are reached, a test may be under-representative of true ability as the test limit has been reached before the limit of the test taker.

Pros and cons of the Stanford-Binet

The Stanford-Binet is one of the oldest intelligence tests in existence and is widely used worldwide. Therefore, its results are generally familiar and accepted in most places. It is also one of the few tests that is able to test children as young as 2, meaning it is often the only choice for those looking to test very young children.

However, the test was last updated in 2003 so is an older revision compared to many of the other tests currently available. This leads some to believe it can overstate IQ due to the Flynn Effect (see page 20).

Although it does have the ability to test young children, it is possible for very young children to obtain an artificially low score simply because they do not have the levels of concentration that are required by the test. For these reasons, the accuracy of IQ scores at the younger age range is often questioned.

Lastly, the way the SB-V is designed to allow testing across a wide variety of ages means that the test has different question sets for different age ranges. This makes it difficult to get an accurate comparison between different ages. However, because it does differentiate between age groups then there is an argument that it provides the most accurate assessment of IQ.

Weschler Intelligence Test for Children (WISC)

History of the test

David Weschler was a Romanian-American psychologist who initially developed an intelligence test for adults known as the Weschler-Bellevue Scale (later the Weschler Adult Intelligence Scale (WAIS)) in 1939.

At the time it was designed, Weschler disagreed with Binet on how certain parts of the intelligence tests were designed. His test sought to address these criticisms. When it was first released, it was an innovative IQ test in so far as it used a point scale concept: Binet gave credit on the test only when a threshold was reached so if the threshold was 3 out of 4, scoring 2 yielded no score. Weschler changed this by allowing points to be assigned to each item which in turn allowed for items to be grouped – in essence, the first subtests; this also allowed for subtest scores and a comparison of strengths and weaknesses in particular areas.

The other area in which Weschler disagreed with Binet was Binet's focus on verbal testing solely. Weschler felt non-verbal was also important and that it would remove language and cultural bias.

Both these areas of change have subsequently been adopted by almost all IQ tests including later revisions of the Stanford-Binet test.

The WISC was an adaptation of the adult scale to create an IQ test specifically for children and the first iteration was produced by Weschler in 1949.

Current version

The current version of the WISC is the WISC-V which was last updated in 2014.

The WISC is currently on its fifth revision. Since its creation in 1949, it has been updated in 1974, 1991, 2003 and 2014.

The current version takes around 45–60 minutes to complete the standard test depending on the pace, age and concentration of the test taker. However, there are further extended test areas which, if completed, can extend the test time to around 3 hours.

Age range

The WISC-V is designed to be sat by children aged between 6 and 16 years of age. Children over 16 generally sit the WAIS and children younger than 6 sit the WPPSI (explained in more detail in the next section).

Score classification

The current version of the WISC uses a different classification of scores than the previous version. The current classifications are shown in the table below. The WISC uses a standard deviation of 15.

IQ Range	IQ Classification
130 and above	Extremely high
120–129	Very high
110–119	High average
90–109	Average
80–89	Low average
70–79	Very low
69 and below	Extremely low

Subtests

The WISC consists of five primary index scales and in order to calculate these, two subtests must be given for each, giving a total of ten subtests.

Seven of these ten subtests are then used in the calculation of an FSIQ.

The five primary index scales are:

- Verbal Comprehension Index (VCI) – this measures the child's ability to reason verbally. The two required subtests for this section are:
    - Similarities – asking how two words are similar.
    - Vocabulary – asking for a definition of a particular word.

- Visual Spatial Index (VSI) – this measures a child's ability to use spatial processing. The two required subtests are:
    - Block design – a timed task asking the child to put red and white blocks into a displayed pattern.
    - Visual puzzles – children look at puzzles in a book and three pieces from a selection which could be used to construct the puzzle.

- Fluid Reasoning Index (FRI) – this measures a child's ability to use inductive and quantitative reasoning. The two required subtests are:
    - Matrix reasoning – children are shown pictures with one square missing and must choose the missing piece from five options.
    - Figure weights – children view a picture of scales with an object on one side and must choose what should go on the other side to keep the scale balanced.

- Working Memory Index (WMI) – this measures a child's working memory. The two required subtests are:
    - Digit span – children listen to an oral sequence of numbers and then have to repeat them in reverse order and in ascending order.
    - Picture span – children view pictures and then select from provided options to show the pictures they saw, preferably in order.

- Processing Speed Index (PSI) – this measures processing speed. The two required subtests are:
    - Coding – in this timed task, children aged 6–8 mark shapes with lines according to a code; those over 8 use a key to transcribe a digit symbol code.
    - Symbol search – children are given rows of symbols and some target symbols then must determine if the target symbol appears in each row.

As previously mentioned, the WISC uses seven of these subtests to caluclate an FSIQ. The excluded subtests are:
- Visual puzzles
- Picture span
- Symbol search

The remaining subtests results are used in FSIQ calculation with a higher weight given to verbal comprehension and fluid reasoning.

In addition to the five primary index scales and FSIQ, the WISC also includes additional scores which can be calculated for special purposes:

- Quantitative Reasoning Index (QRI)
- Auditory Working Memory Index (AWMI)
- Non-verbal Index (NVI)
- General Ability Index (GAI)
- Cognitive Proficiency Index (CPI).

Of these other indices which can be given as part of the WISC results, the Non-verbal Index (NVI), the General Ability Index (GAI) and the Cognitive Proficiency Index (CPI) can be calculated from the initial subtests.

- NVI is usually calculated when a secondary issue such as an English language learner or an autism spectrum disorder may result in lower performance in verbal tests and therefore underrepresent the FSIQ. In these cases, the NVI can be a more accurate representation of ability.
- GAI is calculated when there is a discrepancy in results specifically where WMI or PSI is lower. This can indicate a secondary underlying condition such as an autism spectrum disorder or ADHD, among others.
- CPI specifically shows how cognitive information is processed whilst problem solving or using higher order reasoning.

The Quantitative Reasoning Index (QRI), and the Auditory Working Memory Index (AWMI) require additional subtests to be taken in the five primary index areas. There are secondary subtests available for this purpose.

- QRI looks specifically at the subtests measuring quantitative reasoning such as arithmetic and figure-based subtests. It is indicative of quantitative reasoning in isolation.
- AWMI looks specifically at auditory working memory rather than visual-spatial working memory.

Ceiling scores

The WISC-V has a FSIQ ceiling of 160 and each subtest has a ceiling score of 19. An average subtest score is considered to be between 8 and 12. What this means is that if your child hits the ceiling on the test or subtests, they could not have scored any higher on that particular test or section regardless of how many more questions they answered. In cases where the ceiling scores are reached, a test may be under-representative of true ability as the test limit has been reached before the limit of the test taker.

However, extended norms are available for the WISC-V. These can be used in cases where a child has reached the ceiling on a subtest. When used, they can extend the ceiling to 28 on subtests and to an FSIQ ceiling of 210.

Not all subtests are able to support ceilings of 28 and particularly when a child is near the upper age range of the WISC-V the ability to effectively use extended norms is reduced. Although they can produce a more accurate FSIQ in highly gifted individuals.

Pros and cons of the WISC-V

The WISC-V is specifically designed for children and therefore can be viewed as a purpose designed tool and, as such, especially fit for purpose.

However, it is important to consider that if a child is of especially high ability and is close to the age of 16, the upper age limit of the test, then the limitations of the test may be reached before the limitations of the test taker and therefore the result will be under-representative of ability. In these cases, it may be better to wait until the child is able to take the WAIS or consider an alternative test.

The variety of indices that can be calculated from the WISC-V allow for secondary conditions to be compensated for and for a more accurate representative IQ figure to be generated in many cases.

The ability of the WISC-V to extend the ceiling scores in some subtests by using extended norms is particularly useful in highly gifted individuals who are likely to hit the ceiling in many of the subtests.

The fact that the WISC-V was updated relatively recently (2014) also means it is less likely to be affected by the Flynn Effect (see page 20) than the SB-V.

If a child is in the lower age range for the test, both the WISC-V and the WPPSI-IV are available options. For high ability children, however, the WISC-V is possibly a better choice as discussed in the next section.

Weschler Preschool and Primary Scale of Intelligence (WPPSI)

History of the test

The WPPSI arose out of the WAIS and the WISC. It was first designed by David Weschler in 1967 as an intelligence test for 4–6-year-olds as the WISC was only designed to test from 6 years of age and Weschler had identified a growing demand for the assessment of preschool age children.

Current version

The current version of the WPPSI is the WPPSI-IV which was last updated in 2012.

The WPPSI is currently on its fourth revision. Since its creation in 1967, it has been updated in 1989, 2002 and 2012.

The current version takes 30–60 minutes to complete the standard test. Generally speaking, the younger the test taker, the shorter the test will be.

Age range

The WPPSI-IV is designed to be sat by children between the ages of 2 years 6 months to 7 years 7 months. There are two separate bands within the WPPSI-IV, one for ages 2 years 6 months to 3 years 11 months and one for ages 4 years to 7 years 7 months. The main differences between the two bands are the subtests involved and these are explained in more detail in the subtest section below. There is an overlap of age bracket between the upper level of the WPPSI-IV at 7 years 7 months and the lower level of the WISC-V at 6 years. Children aged between 6 years and 7 years 7 months can sit either test. However, it is important to consider the reason for sitting the test and base the decision for which one on the child. For children of high ability, it is probably better to sit the WISC-V as they are likely to reach the ceiling of the WPPSI-IV.

Score classifications

The current classifications for the WPPSI-IV are shown in the table below. The WPPSI-IV uses a standard deviation of 15.

IQ Range	IQ Classification
130 and above	Very superior
120–129	Superior
110–119	High average
90–109	Average
80–89	Low average
70–79	Borderline
69 and below	Extremely low

Subtests

The WPPSI-IV gives the ability to provide a FSIQ score, five primary index scale scores plus four further ancillary index scores if all the subtests are completed.

This breadth gives the ability to look at a wide variety of factors across the test, which can be especially useful in cases where exceptionalities other than giftedness are suspected.

The five primary index scores are:

- Verbal Comprehension Index (VCI) – this measures the child's ability to reason verbally.
- Visual Spatial Index (VSI) – this measures a child's ability to use spatial processing.
- Fluid Reasoning Index (FRI) – this measures a child's ability to use inductive and quantitative reasoning. This is only calculated for children aged 4 to 7 years 7 months.
- Working Memory Index (WMI) – this measures a child's working memory.
- Processing Speed Index (PSI) – this measures processing speed. This is only calculated for children aged 4 to 7 years 7 months.

The four ancillary index scales are:

- Vocabulary Acquisition Index (VAI) – looks at the development of vocabulary relative to age. Low scores may indicate that additional evaluation of speech and language acquisition is required.
- Non-verbal Index (NVI) – looks at overall ability on those subtests not requiring verbal responses. It can be helpful if a child has a secondary condition such as impaired hearing or autism spectrum disorder or is an English language learner.
- General Ability Index (GAI) – looks at overall ability with less weight placed on working memory and processing speed. It is helpful if

there is a secondary issue that may artificially lower the FSIQ in these areas.

- Cognitive Proficiency Index (CPI) – looks at how cognitive information is processed using higher order reasoning. This is only calculated for children aged 4 to 7 years 7 months.

The WPPSI-IV has a total of 15 subtests. However, it is divided into two age bands: 2 years 6 months to 3 years 11 months, and 4 years to 7 years 7 months.

Children in the lower age band sit up to seven of these subtests. Five of the subtests are required to assess a FSIQ, whilst a sixth subtest is required to be able to calculate the WMI. An optional seventh subtest can be taken to aid in calculation of the General Ability Index (GAI) and the FSIQ.

The five core subtests required for FSIQ calculation are:

- Receptive vocabulary – this assesses a child's ability to identify a word correctly; for example, they may have to point to the correct picture which shows the word said by the tester.
- Information – this assesses a child's ability to recall facts. It looks at long-term memory and acquired knowledge.
- Block design – this assesses a child's ability to reproduce a picture of a design with actual coloured blocks. It looks at visual processing, dexterity, visual-motor coordination and non-verbal concepts among other things.

- Object assembly – this assesses a child's ability to analyse and complete a basic puzzle using coloured blocks to form an image. It looks at logic and coordination as well as both inductive and deductive reasoning.
- Picture memory – a child looks at pictures for a specified amount of time. They then have to select the pictures from options on the response page. This assesses visual short-term memory.

To calculate the Working Memory Index, a further subtest is required:

- Zoo locations – this assesses a child's ability to recall locations. A child views animal cards laid out in a specific pattern and then must recreate the pattern. This considers visual-spatial memory.

A further additional subtest can be administered to provide more information for the calculation of FSIQ and the GAI (ancillary index scale), however it is not a required subtest and calculations can be made without this:

- Picture naming – this assesses a child's ability to name or otherwise indicate which element of a picture is missing. It looks at their ability to separate essential from non-essential and requires observation.

Children aged 4 to 7 years 7 months can sit up to 15 subtests. Of these 15 tests, 10 are core subtests that must be sat in order to generate the primary index scores. The additional subtests can be used to provide further information and to generate ancillary index scores if required.

The 10 core subtests are as follows (some are identical to those above but have been repeated here for convenience):

- Similarities – this assesses logical thinking and verbal reasoning. A child is shown two similar but different objects/concepts and must explain how they are alike or different.

- Information – this assesses a child's ability to recall facts and tests long-term memory and acquired knowledge.

- Block design – this assesses a child's ability to reproduce a picture of a design with actual coloured blocks. It evaluates visual processing, dexterity, visual-motor coordination and nonverbal concepts among other things.

- Object assembly – this assesses a child's ability to analyse and complete a basic puzzle using coloured blocks to form an image. It evaluates logic and coordination as well as both inductive and deductive reasoning.

- Picture memory – a child looks at pictures for a specified amount of time. They then have to select the pictures from options on the response page. This assesses visual short-term memory.

- Picture concepts – assesses categorical and abstract reasoning. A child is asked to look at two or three rows of pictures and choose which shares characteristics with the single picture from the other rows.

- Zoo locations – assesses a child's ability to recall locations. A child views animal cards laid out in a specific pattern and then must recreate the pattern. This looks at visual-spatial memory.

- Matrix reasoning – this assesses a child's ability to select the most appropriate picture from a selection of four, that fits into the previously provided pattern or sequence. It looks at fluid intelligence, classification, processing and perceptual observation among other things.

- Bug search – this assesses a child's ability to look at a picture of bugs and identify which matches the target picture within a specified amount of time. It looks at short-term visual memory, concentration and cognitive flexibility.

- Cancellation – this assesses a child's ability to mark target objects from two arrangements of object groups, one organised and one random, within a specified time limit. This looks at rate of processing, scanning capacity and visual discrimination and recognition. It requires concentration and recall.

The five additional subtests are:

- Receptive vocabulary – this assesses a child's ability to identify a word correctly; for example, they may have to point to the correct picture which shows the word said by the tester.

- Picture naming – assesses a child's ability to name or otherwise indicate which element of a picture is missing. It looks at ability to separate essential from non-essential and requires observation.

- Animal coding – uses animal pictures and basic shapes. Children use a key to mark only those shapes that correspond to the pictured animals. It assesses non-verbal learning and short-term memory.

- Vocabulary – this assesses a child's ability to name an object pictured or define a word given verbally. It looks at verbal fluency, word knowledge and usage.
- Comprehension – this assesses a child's ability to select a picture that shows the best response to a social situation or general principle or to answer questions based on their general understanding of social situations. It looks at common sense, social maturity and use of practical judgement.

Ceiling scores

The WPPSI-IV has a FSIQ ceiling of 160 and each subtest has a ceiling score of 19. An average subtest score is considered to be between 8 and 12. What this means is that if your child hits the ceiling on the test or subtests, they could not have scored any higher on that particular test or section regardless of how many more questions they answered. In cases where the ceiling scores are reached, a test may be under-representative of true ability as the test limit has been reached before the limit of the test taker.

Pros and cons of WPPSI-IV

The WPPSI-IV has been specifically designed to IQ test young children, therefore, if you are looking at testing a child below the age of around 5, then it can provide a good option. The variety of subtests enable the calculation of various primary and ancillary index scales which can beespecially useful in pointing to potential secondary problems or a more accurate indication of IQ in children with a secondary issue.

However, the fact that it has been designed for use with a small age range, means that children who are highly gifted and towards the upper age range of the WPPSI-IV, may well reach the ceiling of the test and therefore it can be under-representative of actual ability. In these cases, it is perhaps better to consider waiting until the child is of an age to sit the WISC-V or to consider the SB-V as an alternative.

Woodcock-Johnson Tests of Cognitive Ability

History of the test

The Woodcock Johnson Test of Cognitive Ability (WJTCA) was first developed in 1979 by American psychometrician Richard Woodcock and Mary Bonner Johnson. It was the first test of its kind to be developed in tandem with a test of achievement.

When taken together, the WJTCA and the Woodcock-Johnson Test of Achievement can provide information on both the cognitive potential of an individual and the actual level of academic achievement and cognitive development. Subsequent developments of the tests have seen a third test added to the co-normed group – The Woodcock Johnson Test of Oral Language which can provide an understanding of an individual's strengths and weaknesses with expressive language.

Current version

The current version of the WJTCA is the WTCJA-IV which was last updated in 2014.

The WJTCA is currently on its fourth revision. Since its creation in 1979, it has been updated in 1989, 2001 and 2014.

There is no recommended time for test completion and the tester can also choose to administer elements of other Woodcock Johnson tests if so indicated – for example, tests from the Woodcock Johnson Test of Achievement. This flexibility means that the amount of time required for the test can vary quite considerably.

Age range

The WJTCA is designed to be sat by people aged 2 to 90. It has been normed for use within this age range.

Score classification

The current classifications of the WJTCA are shown in the table below. The WJTCA uses a standard deviation of 15.

IQ Range	IQ Classification
131 and above	Very superior
121–130	Superior
111–120	High average
90–110	Average
80–89	Low average
70–79	Low
69 and below	Very low

The WJTCA can be scored either on an age-equivalent or a school grade-equivalent basis depending on the age of the test taker and the reasons for the test. If scored on an age-equivalent basis, the report will indicate an age level for the test taker's average performance on a task – e.g. "performing at a 12 year 1 month level". For grade-equivalent scoring, the report will indicate a grade level for the test taker's average performance on a task – e.g. "performing at a 7th grade level".

Subtests

The WJTCA consists of ten subtests in the Standard Battery and a further eight subtests in the Extended Battery. By using the scores obtained in the subtests, factor scores can be calculated that indicate ability in specific areas. The Standard Battery can provide a FSIQ score (termed a General Ability Index or G score by the WJTCA) as well as a further four factor scores:

- Comprehension Knowledge (Gc)
- Fluid Reasoning (Gf)
- Short-term Working Memory (Gwm)
- Gf/Gc Composite (GfGc)

The GfGc was introduced for the first time in the fourth revision of the WJTCA. As it combines crystallised knowledge with fluid reasoning, it gives a highly accurate overview of an individual's strengths and weaknesses across multiple areas. It can be especially useful to highlight any underlying issues.

The Standard Battery of tests is comprehensive enough to provide a good overview and understanding of the cognitive abilities of an individual. The Extended Battery can be used to provide more depth and additional information. It can also be particularly useful if there are secondary conditions that may need to be accounted for in an individual.

The Extended Battery can be used to provide a further six factor scores:

- Cognitive Processing Speed (Gs)
- Auditory Processing (Ga)
- Long-term Retrieval (Glr)
- Visual Processing (Gv)
- Number Facility (N)
- Perceptual Speed (P)

The subtests in the Standard Battery are:

- Verbal attention – this assesses a child's ability to repeat items in order after listening to a recorded list of numbers and animals. It looks at working memory, recall and attention span.
- Phonological processing – this subtest is broken into three smaller subtests. Overall, the subtests look at auditory processing, cognitive flexibility and speed of word access/recall. The subtests are:
  - Word access – the child listens to a recording of an alphabet sound and must then say a word that starts, ends or has the sound in the middle as directed.
  - Word fluency – the child is required to name as many words as they can recall.
  - Substitution – the child is required to substitute a word, a word-ending or a letter sound as directed, to make a new word.
- Story recall – this assesses a child's ability to recall as many details as possible in increasingly complex stories. It looks at short-term memory and auditory working memory.

- Visualisation – this subtest is broken into two smaller subtests. Overall, they look at visual stimuli and visual working memory. The two subtests are:
    - Spatial relations – the child views shapes made of puzzle pieces; they are subsequently shown individual puzzle pieces and must determine which belong in the shape shown previously.
    - Block rotation – the child is shown a 3-D pattern of blocks. They are then shown five similar block patterns and must identify which of the two are rotated versions of the initial pattern.
- General information – this assesses a child's ability to answer questions about general surroundings and general knowledge such as 'where would you find …' or 'what does … do'. It looks at acquired knowledge and ability to use expressive language.
- Concept formation – this assesses a child's ability to determine rules for an item based on a complete stimulus set. It looks at fluid reasoning, deductive reasoning and working memory.
- Numbers reversed – this assesses a child's ability to repeat a given sequence of numbers in reverse order. It looks at auditory working memory.
- Oral vocabulary – this assesses a child's ability to provide synonyms and antonyms for spoken words. It looks at word knowledge and expressive language.

- Number series – this assesses a child's ability to provide the missing number from a pattern or series. This looks at fluid reasoning, deduction and working memory.
- Letter-pattern matching – this assesses a child's ability to identify and mark two identical letters in rows of six letters within an allotted time span. It looks at processing speed.

The additional subtests in the Extended Battery are:

- Number-pattern matching – this assesses a child's ability to identify and mark two identical numbers in rows of six numbers within an allotted time span. It looks at processing speed.
- Non-word repetition – this assesses a child's ability to listen to a recording and then repeat phonetic or common language component patterns that are not words. It looks at recall and working memory.
- Visual-auditory learning – this assesses a child's ability to view symbols which are associated with a word given orally; the child must then look at a sequence of symbols and repeat the sentence given based on the word related to each symbol. It looks at auditory association and recall.
- Picture recognition – this assesses a child's ability to recognise pictures from a larger group which match pictures shown previously. It looks at visual spatial processing and visual memory.
- Analysis-synthesis – this assesses a child's ability to process and follow instructions to perform a complex procedure. It looks at deductive reasoning, cognitive flexibility and fluid reasoning.

- Object-number sequencing – this assesses a child's ability to listen to a recording of objects and numbers and then repeat the numbers in sequence, followed by the objects in sequence. It looks at working memory and cognitive flexibility.
- Pair cancellation – this assesses a child's ability to find and mark a particular pattern as many times as possible within a given time frame. It looks at recall and attention span.
- Memory for words – this assesses a child's ability to listen to and then repeat in sequence a list of unrelated words. It looks at verbal memory and attention span.

Ceiling scores

The WJTCA is especially flexible in its approach to scoring and allows for FSIQ scores as high as 200. Each individual subtest has its own ceiling score and a trigger for that ceiling (for example, 10 incorrect answers may be considered a ceiling in a particular test). Since the test is designed for an extended age range, there is good scope for a child to continue answering questions until they reach their natural ceiling as opposed to reaching the limitation of the test itself.

Pros and cons of the WJTCA

The WJTCA is just one component of the WJ-IV selection of tests. If taken alone, the WJTCA can produce a good understanding of IQ and cognitive potential. However, if taken alongside the other tests of achievement and oral language, it can show a very complete picture of cognitive ability and current academic achievement level.

Since it is designed for a wide age range and has a flexibility built into the ceiling scores, the ceilings are generous enough to allow for relatively accurate results.

The WJTCA has one standard calculation for FSIQ which is accepted by the majority of organisations. Whilst it has other factor scores that are calculated, these are often not accepted as FSIQ scores for the purposes of entry into organisations such as Mensa. In contrast, organisations often accept the WISC and the WPPSI scores of either FSIQ or GAI which means in the case of an underlying condition where FSIQ can be under-represented, the WISC or WPPSI may be a better choice.

Choosing a test

As you can see, there are many IQ test options and each has its pros and cons, meaning some may be better suited to your circumstances than others. Be aware that not all psychologists and testing professionals will administer all tests so discuss with your chosen provider about which test will be the best suited to your child and it may be that you might need to find a different provider to administer that particular test.

Another thing to consider when deciding on an IQ test is the language in which to take the test if you are a non-native English speaker. The verbal components of IQ tests may be more problematic if taken in a second language and therefore impact the overall score. A second consideration is not just the language of the test but also the cultural norms and references within the test. For these reasons, IQ tests have been translated into different languages but also have different editions within the same language – i.e. an Australasian edition, a British edition, a North American edition, etc. When deciding on IQ tests, talk to your preferred provider about which version of a test may be best and if it is not available in your testing country, make sure you understand if this will have any effect on the scores.

What is working memory?

Working memory is one of the brain's executive functioning skills. It allows the brain to store information temporarily until it is needed. It allows the brain to keep hold of information while not losing track of what is being done at the time. This information may not be stored, or the brain may use the working memory to help organise information for long-term storage.

4

Results – What Do They Really Mean?

So, you have decided to go down the testing route and now you have the report and confirmation that your child is gifted – but now what? What does this really mean?

Again, and like with most things gifted that are discussed in this book, it depends! In chapter 1, we considered different definitions of giftedness and came to understand some of the characteristics and physical attributes of giftedness. However, we did not discuss numbers or IQ scores. For some people who choose not to IQ test, they may never have a number or score but be able to be identified as gifted through their characteristics or behaviour.

Having an IQ score is not a prerequisite for giftedness, all it does is verify what may already be known or at least suspected. For this reason, I deliberately avoided gifted classification as a particular IQ score in my earlier discussion on the definition of giftedness. It is nonetheless a useful tool if you have an IQ test score and the numbers can help us to understand a little more about giftedness in general and your child's giftedness in particular.

The first thing to understand is that giftedness is not one-size-fits-all. It is possible to classify giftedness as any IQ score over 130 but as we shall discuss, this is too simplistic a definition.

Let's take a look at a bell curve to understand how IQ scores work and what this means in reality. An IQ test plots scores on a standard bell curve and for most IQ tests, this bell curve has a standard deviation of 15.

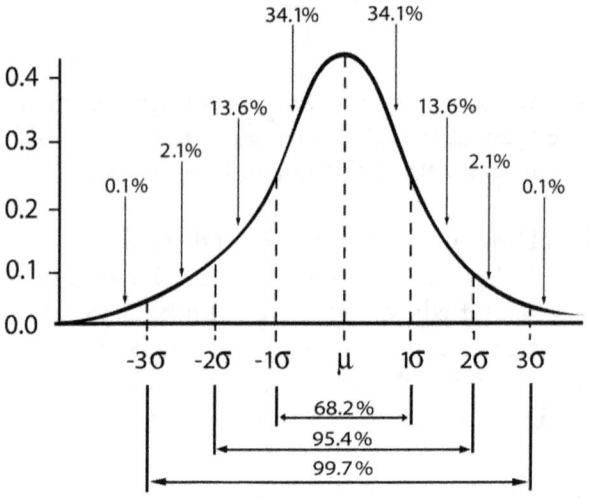

Bell curve showing standard deviations and percentages

The average IQ for these tests is deemed to be 100 and, when the tests are reissued, they are generally normed to 100.

This means that 68% of the population should have an IQ within one standard deviation of the norm – so 68% of the population would be expected to receive a score between 85–115 on a correctly administered IQ test. This is generally considered to be an average IQ.

Of the remaining 32%, half will have IQs greater than 115 and half will have IQs lower than 85. Scores of greater than 115 occur in around 16% of the population.

An IQ of 130 is two standard deviations from the mean and will occur in less than 2% of the population. This is generally accepted as a gifted IQ under all definitions. Mensa, for example, requires an IQ of at least 130 for membership.

However, some organisations and school districts may classify giftedness as being the top 10% of a population – i.e. using Gagné's definition (see page 6). Using the bell curve, this would put a gifted IQ at anything above 120.

It is useful to put these scores into some sort of context to get a better understanding of what a particular IQ score really means. Obviously, the higher the score, and the closer to the tail of the bell curve, the fewer instances occur but what does this mean in practice?

Here it is helpful to look at the rarity of IQ scores among the population as a 1 in X number.

The table below shows gifted IQ scores with their percentile rank and rarity among the population. For example, looking at the table below you can see that an IQ score of 145 puts a person ahead of 99.87% of the population in terms of IQ and this happens in 1 in every 741 people.

IQ Score	SD Percentile (SD=15)	Rarity (1:X)
119	89.74%	10
120	90.87%	11
125	95.22%	21
130	97.72%	44
135	99.02%	102
140	99.62%	261
145	99.87%	741
150	99.96%	2330
155	99.99%	8137
156	99.99%	10,581
157	99.99%	13,817
158	99.99%	18,120
159	99.99%	23,863
160	99.99%	31,560

An SD of 15 has been used as this is the most common among IQ tests. As the current versions of many IQ tests have a ceiling of 160, the table stops at this point.

As you can see, because the bell curve tails off, the scores towards the tails of the bell curve happen in an increasingly small percentage of the population. It also magnifies the effect of additional points. So, for example, an IQ of 120 happens in 1 in every 11 people whereas an IQ of 125 happens in 1 in every 21 people so the rarity is nearly doubled with the increase of five IQ points. An IQ of 150 happens in 1 in every 2,330 people whereas an IQ of 155 happens in 1 in every 8,137 people so the rarity is nearly four times greater with the increase of five IQ points at this point.

The table above highlights the rarity of higher IQ and goes someway to illuminating why it is important to recognise degrees of giftedness. All the IQ tests do this in their reports and the tables for the tests discussed in this book can be found in chapter 3. However, like so many things within this field, there is no standard terminology and different tests use different words to indicate different levels of IQ.

Like many things surrounding giftedness, there are differences of classification and opinion about how to categorise giftedness. A lot of the discrepancy also comes because prior to the most current revisions of the IQ tests, the ceilings and scoring were somewhat different and it was possible to get IQ scores of 200. In the current revisions of the tests, most have a ceiling score of 160. This means that it is difficult to map or categorise IQ scores between people who took previous test versions, and people who took the current version.

Since this book is looking mostly at gifted children and the beginnings of the journey, I am going to ignore the earlier versions of the test on the basis that most reading this book are likely to have undergone testing since the latest revisions.

Therefore, I use the following classifications of giftedness based on an amalgamation of classifications from several sources including the Davidson Institute, Hoagie's Gifted and Ruf's Levels of Giftedness and adjusted to account for the changes between the current versions of IQ tests and the older versions capping the potential score at 160 on an IQ test:

Level of Giftedness	IQ Range
Mildly gifted	120–129
Moderately gifted	130–138
Highly gifted	139–145
Exceptionally gifted	146–152
Profoundly gifted	153–160

But we now need to understand how this manifests in abilities and characteristics and start to get a better understanding of what the different levels of giftedness really mean and why they are important. Here, it is useful to turn to the work of Dr Deborah Ruf.

Dr Deborah Ruf started her career as an elementary school teacher but moved into the field of gifted education after becoming a parent of gifted children. She attained a PhD in Educational Psychology and her doctorate looked at the lives of 41 gifted adults. She identified five levels of giftedness which she has broken down and categorised quite extensively. Let's have a brief look at these levels to try to get an understanding for degrees of giftedness and why it matters.

Below is a description of each of the levels of giftedness Dr Ruf highlights. However, keep in mind that the examples given are indications of what giftedness might look like at that level – it is not exhaustive or exclusive. There is also some overlap in IQ scores and terminology between levels.

Level One

- IQ range of roughly 120–129. Often termed superior on IQ tests.
- Can find around 6–8 students per class in this range – around a quarter of all students.
- Show early interest in colours, numbers, letters, often before 2 years old.
- Have a good vocabulary and sentence structure by age 3.
- Can do some basic addition and subtraction by age 4.
- Reading confidently by 6 years old and reading chapter books by age 7.

Level Two

- IQ range of 130–135. (There can be some overlap between the levels at the top and bottom of the ranges). Often termed very superior on IQ tests.
- Can usually find one or two other students in this range in a classroom.
- Show an early interest in being read to and pay attention to the story; even turn pages by 15 months.
- Recognise letters by 18 months and colours by 20 months.
- Some start reading by age 4 and usually independent readers by age 6.
- Start counting objects in groups between ages 3–4.

Level Three

- IQ range of 136–140. Often termed very superior on IQ tests.
- Often only one or two other students in this range per 100 students in a school.
- Alert from a very young age – looking round the room and focusing on faces and voices.
- Love being read to and pay attention to stories by around 10–12 months.
- Have memorised favourite books by age 2.
- Very competent talkers who ask lots of questions by age 3.
- Can do addition, subtraction and count backwards by age 3. Some have progressed to multiplication, division and fractions by age 6.
- Can read often before they start school.

Level Four

- IQ of 141+ Often termed very advanced on IQ tests.
- Often only one or two students in this range per 200 students in a school.
- Hyper-alert at a very young age.
- Strong interest in books and being read to by 3–4 months.
- Mastered the alphabet by 15–21 months.
- Read fluently and independently for pleasure by age 5.
- Speak in complex sentences with a large vocabulary by age 2.

Level Five
- IQ of 145+ Often termed highly advanced on IQ tests.
- Very infrequent in the population so may be the only one at this level in the school.
- Speak in full complex sentences by age 2.
- Read spontaneously and for pleasure by age 4–5.
- Understand relatively complex maths problems by age 4.
- Have existential concerns and may question the existence of Santa and the Tooth Fairy by age 4.

It is important to remember that although a lot of the discussion above focuses on an IQ score, it is also possible to get an understanding of your child's level of giftedness from the traits and characteristics discussed. You do not have to have had a formal IQ test done.

Looking at Dr Ruf's levels of giftedness along with an understanding of the bell curve of the IQ tests demonstrates why it is important to not only identify a child as gifted, but to identify the level of giftedness as well. The speed of knowledge acquisition and the prevalence of others in a similar classification differs across the levels. As we can see from the bell curve, the further towards the tail you get, the more infrequent the instance. So, as seen in Ruf's Levels of Giftedness, a child at level one may find several others at a similar level within the same environment whereas a child at level five may not find anyone with a similar profile in the entire school.

Just as we are looking at how a gifted child differs from a neurotypical child – how a child with an IQ of 100 is different from a child with an IQ of 130 – so too is a gifted child with an IQ of 160 different from a gifted child with an IQ of 130.

So, not only must we, as parents, understand that our children are gifted but we must also understand where on the gifted scale they lie as we can begin to identify where they are most likely to feel frustrations and where we need to direct our efforts to support them. We will discuss what this looks like in the following chapter.

5

So Where Do We Go From Here?

Hopefully you now have an understanding of what being gifted really means and you also probably have an idea of your child's level of giftedness, either through formal testing or through a review of your child's abilities and when they hit milestones. The big question now is how to use that knowledge to help your child.

One of the biggest things that struck me when I was trying to figure out how to help my child, was that so much of the literature and studies regarding gifted children suggest that you need to parent differently. That your child will have particular needs that may be different to neurotypical children and therefore, these need to be addressed in how you parent. The main difficulty I had with that statement is that the whole discussion and explanation around giftedness also explains that all gifted children are different – so, how exactly do you know what specific needs your child has and how you can best help them?

Well, the answer I think is that it will take time. You will be going on this journey with your child and as you travel along it, you will start to identify particular areas, issues or characteristics that are attributable to giftedness. But, to get there on your own will be very challenging. So, one of the best things you can do now is to try to find other gifted children and parents. This can be easy in some places or more difficult if you live in a more isolated location; but even if you don't have anyone physically close by, you can access various gifted communities online. It's likely preferable, if possible, to connect with people who live in the same country as you. This is because every country has different approaches and options available to gifted children when it comes to schooling and by accessing communities in your area, having experienced the local systems and processes, they will be better placed to help answer any questions you may have.

While all gifted children are unique, there are traits that are more common and talking things through with other parents, especially those that are further into the journey, can help to open your eyes to those characteristics in your child. Parenting a gifted child can be a challenge, and support groups are a really great way to help you through this challenge in the most effective way, to achieve the outcome we all want – a happy child.

Support groups

The first place to look can be official gifted organisations such as Mensa or the International High IQ Society (if your child is older than 15). These organisations are worldwide and require your child to have an IQ score in the top 2–5%, depending on the society, as a requirement for entry. Mensa in particular is divided by country or region and therefore you are more likely to be able to connect with people who are close by. Many Mensa chapters also run events dedicated to children and you can therefore meet other parents and gifted children in your area this way.

Another avenue to explore is social media and Facebook groups dedicated to gifted children. There are many such groups, a lot of them specific to local areas but some global ones as well. There are some which require your child to be IQ tested as gifted and some which allow you entry even on the impression of giftedness. The great thing about these groups is that they are a safe space to ask questions and to learn from the experiences of other parents as well. Many of the groups also help each other out by posting useful documents, research papers, booklists, and even suggested activities in the files section of the group page. Some also have some members willing to act as mentors to other members and these can be found under the mentorship tab of the group page. It is well worth looking to see if you can find a group local to your area, but also to look at joining some of the worldwide groups as well as this can give you a wider base of knowledge and shared experience. At the time of writing, these Facebook groups were open to people globally:

- Parents of Gifted & High Ability Children
- Parenting Gifted or Advanced Children
- Hoagies Gifted Discussion Group
- Parenting Gifted Preschoolers (ages 2–5)
- Parents of Gifted and Twice-Exceptional Kids

Global organisations

Depending on where in the world you live, there may also be other organisations specifically aimed at supporting and encouraging gifted children and their parents. Most countries will have an organisation that you can join but the level of support and access provided can differ. Some provide mainly academic resources and a few seminars whereas some provide a full service of support to children and parents.

Below are just a few of these organisations, but of course there are likely to be more! Facebook groups and Mensa in your area may also be able to point you in the direction of support organisations in your area if one is not listed here.

United States of America (USA)

The Davidson Young Scholars programme is open to children aged 5–16 who are citizens or permanent residents of the USA and have a score of 145+ on a properly administered IQ test. The Young Scholar programme is free and provides support, holiday programmes and a community of like-minded people.

There are a number of other organisations in the USA which are also very good at supporting gifted children as well as a number of organisations that run courses and events for gifted children. Many of these are state-specific so check with your local Facebook group or Mensa for other possibilities near you.

United Kingdom (UK)

Potential Plus UK provides support and guidance for parents and gifted children. There is no specified requirement for entry although a fee is payable – ranging from £60–125 per year depending on the level of support required. They also provide unlimited telephone support for free in certain memberships or for £36 per half hour for non-members.

Hong Kong

The Hong Kong Academy for Gifted Education offers information, support and learning experiences to children aged 10–18. It also offers support and training opportunities to parents and teachers. To enter the programme as a gifted child, you need to be nominated and complete an assessment although a formal IQ test result is not required. Fees vary depending on which elements/workshops are chosen.

Australia

The Australian Association for the Education of the Gifted and Talented (AAEGT) looks to further the understanding of gifted children throughout the education sector in Australia. They run events and publish a journal; but many of the support or academic opportunities for parents and children are run by state organisations. These are usually affliated to AAEGT so you should be able to find your local state association vias the AAEGT website or by talking with them directly.

New Zealand

The New Zealand Association for Gifted Children looks to support parents, children and professionals through advocacy to the education sector, they provide some short courses and workshops as well as a library of resources. They also help support parents to set up local branches to connect gifted children.

South Africa

Gifted Children South Africa look to support gifted children and parents in understanding what it means to be gifted by providing support and resources.

Telling others

Whether or not you tell other people about your child is of course completely up to you. However, just remember that there is often a lack of understanding regarding giftedness. Many feel giftedness is synonymous with academic achievement and may feel that you are bragging. I would suggest that you think carefully about who you are talking to. If you think they will be receptive, then perhaps look to educate them on what giftedness really is so that they understand and can support your child (and you!). For those that might not be so receptive to a lesson in giftedness, just think about how you will explain things and, equally, if you really need to.

It is unfortunate but I know of several people who have had very negative experiences with friends not understanding the nature of the challenge posed by having a gifted child. Often, they feel it is an entirely positive thing and don't fully understand the unique challenges involved. Also, I have found that gifted can be an evocative and misunderstood word. I usually address this with others by saying that my child needs extension and some specialist help in school rather than by describing him as gifted. I have found that this seems to be more understood and accepted. However, everyone will have different experiences and you may well find that this isn't an issue.

Encouraging your gifted child

Now that you understand your child is gifted, and are beginning to discover what that means, you may be starting to understand your gifted child a little more. You may be discovering their strengths and weakness, likes and dislikes. My advice is to try to find a way to embrace this and use the knowledge to encourage your child. I found that my child was interested in things that would be considered non-typical at an early age. For example, one of his favourite things to do at age 4 was sums! He would ask us to write addition, subtraction or division problems and would want us to make them complicated to "trick him". Often, he would ask to do this in favour of playing on a playground or colouring or another activity which seemed more appropriate at 4 years of age. I worried that we were not allowing him to be a child or that he was feeling pressure to do these activities and I would try to get him to do other more age-appropriate things. What I realised once I started to understand giftedness a little more is that he genuinely derived pleasure from these activities. Once I had understood this, it became easier to encourage him in these interests although I do try to ensure I am guided by him and don't pressure him.

Unfortunately, this is one area where you may find some resistance from others – friends, teachers, etc. I have sometimes found that allowing a child to pursue academic interests can be frowned upon and you may be considered a pushy parent. Yet, if you were to expect your child to spend hours a week on a soccer field or doing ballet, this would be more accepted. Neither interest – academic nor athletic – should be more worthy than the other. If your child is interested in pursuing an activity, let them do it!

The key thing about gifted children is that they often have a strong curiosity and desire to learn. Embrace this, encourage it and try to find ways they can grow in these areas. This might mean throwing preconceptions out the window and buying your child seemingly boring educational birthday presents – my child asked for a globe and a telescope for his fifth birthday. It might mean finding coding groups or science clubs. It might mean encouraging development in a particular sport or a second language from an early age. Whatever it is, encourage and support it.

This is particularly useful advice if your child is not yet at school or isn't being challenged in a school environment. By stretching and challenging them in areas of interest outside of a school environment you give them the opportunity to turn potential into ability.

Likewise, it is important to remember that gifted children often exhibit asynchronous development and just as it is important to support the areas they are keen to explore and develop, so too is it important to challenge them to grow in those areas they are not so strong in. For example, if a child isn't particularly strong athletically, look at alternative ways of developing coordination and fitness. Rather than focusing on more traditional school sports, perhaps look at individual or disciplined sports such as swimming, trampolining, parkour, gymnastics or martial arts and see if one of these pique their interest.

Supporting the social and emotional child

One of the common struggles with gifted children is supporting them socially and emotionally. As we have discussed, giftedness is often synonymous with asynchronous development and frequently this asynchronicity is in social and emotional development.

One of the greatest challenges for gifted children, especially with social development, is accessing children of a similar mindset. Depending on the level of giftedness of the child, this can be tricky. If you recall the discussion of Ruf's Levels of Giftedness from the previous chapter, the more gifted a child, the less likely they are to find similar children in a school or local society. Think back to the bell curve again: 68% of the population is likely to have an IQ of between 85–115. So, if you fall within this range, which is completely normal, then you have a large range of other people you can access who share a similar level of IQ. Think now about moving to two or three standard deviations above the mean; a child with an IQ of 130 is in the top 2% of the population. A child with an IQ of 145 is in the top 0.1% of the population, and a child with an IQ of 156 or greater is in the top 0.01% of the population. This makes the likelihood of them finding similar aged peers far more remote.

It is not a lost cause though, despite the statistics! Support groups, as discussed above, will help you to find similar children. Also, gifted children often gravitate towards older children when seeking friendships in a school environment. This makes sense if you think about it: if an exceptionally gifted child is operating two years above their chronological age, then their interests and abilities are perhaps more likely to be aligned with neurotypical children two years older than them, than with those of their own age.

6

The Big Question – Schooling!

One of the biggest concerns around having a gifted child is schooling. After all, schooling forms a huge part of a child's development and takes up a substantial amount of their childhood. You want it to be a nurturing, challenging and happy environment. Unfortunately, gifted children often struggle with conventional schooling and finding a fit can be a task that takes up a lot of your time as the parent of a gifted child. It is also perhaps one of the most daunting tasks you will have to deal with as well.

Gifted children have high cognitive potential. This means that in the right learning environment they often learn faster and with fewer repetitions that a neurotypical child. But it is crucial to remember that giftedness is cognitive *potential* – a gifted child is not born knowing all the times tables, they must still learn this, just often at a faster rate than neurotypical peers. Gifted children also have the potential to add more knowledge than a neurotypical child each year. A gifted child may master twelve or fifteen new concepts in a year whilst a neurotypical child may only master ten. This also means that the gap between a gifted child and a neurotypical age peer can widen each year. So, it is important to try to ensure a school environment that goes at the right pace for a gifted child.

Let's take a look at why this can be such a challenge. Firstly, if you have gone along the road of testing then you will have seen a psychologist or a specialist to administer the test; these professionals generally understand giftedness – that's why they do what they do! If you have found support groups or joined other gifted organisations, you will also have found yourself among people that understand the challenges and nuances of being gifted and parenting gifted children. In essence, you have found supportive environments. That is great, and absolutely necessary! But, unless you are lucky enough to live near one of the few schools specifically catering for gifted children, you may find it a different environment when looking at schools.

Schools, by their design, cater to a broad range of abilities with the focus on the average ability for the age range of the students in the class. Generally, you should expect a teacher to be able to offer a degree of differentiation to children that need either a little extra help or a little extra challenge. Where it gets difficult with gifted children is that they often need a huge amount of additional challenge and this can be difficult to provide within an ordinary classroom. Again, it often depends on the level of giftedness of your child.

The diagram below shows the degree of differentiation often needed in a school environment grows with the increase in IQ. However, conversely, the number of students at that level shrinks with the growth of IQ.

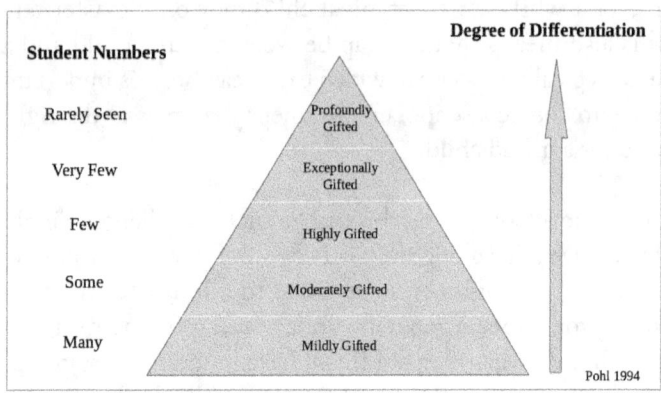

Pohl 1994

This highlights just how challenging it can be for a teacher to adequately cater for a gifted child, particularly an exceptionally gifted or profoundly gifted child. When you factor in that gifted children often show asynchronous behaviour then it becomes even more difficult to find the right place for them to fit within the conventional schooling environment. But it can be done! There are a number of options open to gifted children and as long as you find a school who is willing to work with you then there is no reason why you can't find a method of education that works for your child.

It is, however, important to understand that there is often no single perfect solution when raising a gifted child; asynchronous development and other factors mean that it is often impossible to find a solution which solves all the issues. What you need to look for is the best possible solution – one that solves the majority of issues, or at least the key issues.

In this chapter, I will go through some of the options that may be available to you. The exact choices will depend on where you live, what the legal requirements are for education and how willing the school is to work with you. These are just a guide and there is no one-size-fits-all so it may take a bit of trial and error before you find the right solution for you.

Acceleration

The principal thing to talk about when it comes to schools and finding the right fit is acceleration. It is often the first thing to jump to and often supported or suggested by a psychologist. That said, like everything else in the world of gifted children, it is not that simple, but it is a good place to start a discussion of options.

In 2004, Dr Miraca Gross of the University of New South Wales and Drs Susan Assouline and Nicholas Colangelo of the Belin-Blank Center for Gifted Education and Talent Development at the University of Iowa authored a publication entitled *A Nation Deceived: How Schools Hold Back America's Brightest Students*. This work has had a lasting and positive impact on the understanding of gifted children within education. It is so seminal partly because they addressed common myths and misconceptions towards acceleration and explained in plain English why these did not hold true. The work removed many barriers to understanding and it is still hailed as one of the most influential works in gifted and acceleration research.

Acceleration is one of the most researched yet underutilised tools for gifted children. A large part of that is due to the misconception that acceleration is grade skipping, i.e. when a child skips a year of school and jumps from, for example, year 1 to year 3. This is not the case. Grade skipping is just one way in which acceleration can be utilised for a gifted child. Often when discussing acceleration, people immediately jump to grade skipping so it is worth understanding that this is often the assumption but does not always have to be the solution. It is therefore worth clarifying exactly what is meant by acceleration if the term is used by a psychologist or a school.

In *A Nation Deceived*, the authors define acceleration as moving at a faster pace through the traditional school curriculum. They also point out that there are more than 20 identified types of acceleration. These are:

1. Early admission to kindergarten
2. Early admission to first grade
3. Grade skipping
4. Continuous progress
5. Self-paced instruction
6. Subject matter acceleration/partial acceleration
7. Combined classes
8. Curriculum compacting
9. Telescoping curriculum
10. Mentoring
11. Extracurricular programmes
12. Distance learning courses
13. Concurrent/dual enrolment
14. Advanced Placement
15. International Baccalaureate

16. Accelerated/Honours high school/STEM residential high school
17. Credit by examination
18. Early entrance into middle school, high school or college
19. Early graduation from high school or college
20. Acceleration in college

An initial glance at this list might make you think that not all of these are acceleration and in fact you may have talked about these options but not realised they are types of acceleration.

In essence, you could argue that since gifted children are often further ahead or learn at a faster pace than neurotypical children, then any successful form of education for them has to involve some element of faster progression – therefore some form of acceleration.

One of the biggest and most lasting impacts of *A Nation Deceived* is its discussion of the myths surrounding acceleration. Here we will take a look at just a few of them but it is definitely worth reading the full publication (a link to the available download is in the resources section at the back of the book).

Myth #1: Gifted students don't need help – they'll do fine on their own.

This is not true. If we look back to our initial discussion on a definition of giftedness, you can start to see why this is a myth, and in fact can be harmful to a gifted child. If we consider Renzulli's Three Ring Concept of Giftedness, he specifically states that high potential individuals may only turn this potential into talent if their environment encourages it. Giftedness looks at the potential a child has, not their specific academic ability. A gifted child often has the potential to learn at a faster rate and will grasp concepts faster than their neurotypical peers – but they are not born with the understanding of all these concepts; they still need to be taught them. The real danger with this myth is that if special provisions are not made for gifted children within the classroom, this can have a detrimental effect on their learning as they may disengage through boredom or not learn how to deal with failure. (Both these issues are discussed in further detail in the following chapter.)

Myth #2: Teachers challenge all students so the regular classroom is appropriate.

This is not true across the board for gifted children but the degree to which it is not true depends on the level of giftedness of the child. Have another look at the diagram on page 72. It shows that as the level of giftedness increases, so does the degree of differentiation required. However, as we have discussed previously, gifted children are often asynchronous so a child who is mildly gifted from a FSIQ point of view, may still be far ahead of neurotypical peers in one area of particular interest. What this means is that whilst it is true that teachers do challenge all students, the sheer size of the gap between a neurotypical child and a gifted child may mean that the teacher does not have the time or capacity to challenge to the extent needed without compromising the teaching of the other students. This could be in one subject or across the board, dependent on the level of giftedness and the child.

Myth #3: Gifted students should be in the regular classroom to help other students and to be a good role model.

This is not true. Gifted students should be placed where is best for them, not where might be best for other students at the expense of the gifted child. It also often occurs the other way round and gifted children in inappropriate class placement often exhibit the chameleon effect – where they change their personalities and hide their abilities in order to fit in. They may also become disruptive through boredom. This is the exact opposite of what the myth suggests.

Myth #4: All children are gifted.

This is not true. All children are special and valuable and deserving of the best possible education, but not all children are gifted as defined herein. Looking back at our discussion of the definition of giftedness, it is not academic ability but something else – the potential and natural ability that places gifted children above 90% of the population. The research into physical differences in gifted brains also categorically shows that not everyone is gifted.

Gifted children deserve the best education they can get, just like any other child. The simple fact is gifted children are different from neurotypical children and therefore will require adaptations in the normal educational system in order to succeed.

One of the most significant issues surrounding acceleration is the lack of understanding. In most countries, teacher training does not cover gifted children, so teachers are often not taught to understand, identify and teach gifted children. The myths and assumption that acceleration is equal to grade skipping also means that many educators are against it. Where *A Nation Deceived* has been so helpful is by pointing out these issues and by trying to open eyes to the fact that acceleration is far more than just grade skipping and can be tailored to a child.

A Nation Empowered

In 2015, a follow up report to *A Nation Deceived* was published. *A Nation Empowered: Evidence Trumps the Excuses holding Back America's Brightest Students* looks at the changes that had occurred in education and the catering for gifted students within the school environment. The authors concluded that things had improved, but there was still plenty of room for more growth. (A link to *A Nation Empowered* is available in the resources section of this book.)

The key takeaway from acceleration is to understand exactly how acceleration could work for your child and what form it could take.

So let's look at some of the types of acceleration in more detail as options that could be available to your child. Since the different types of acceleration are not commonly known among schools, I will also use other terminology more common in school environments and highlight the links to the types of acceleration discussed in *A Nation Deceived*.

Extension

Extension is often used as a first attempt to cater for gifted students within the school environment and can be the solution for some children. This can take many forms, namely:

- Continuous progress
- Self-paced instruction
- Subject matter acceleration/partial acceleration
- Compacted curriculum
- Telescoping curriculum
- Mentoring
- Extracurricular programmes
- Concurrent/dual enrolment
- Acceleration in college

In essence, extension often keeps children within their age peer classroom but offers different work to ensure that children are challenged. This can be done in a variety of ways and will depend on how advanced the gifted child is.

It can be possible for a teacher to provide extension simply by requiring more or giving harder problems; for example, a child could be given more challenging spelling words, be asked to write more or given 3-digit maths problems instead of 1- or 2-digits. In this way, a child can learn the principals of whatever subject is being taught, but be asked to use those tools in a more appropriately challenging way. This would be a sort of **continuous progress** or **self-paced instruction**, where a child is being allowed to progress and not waiting on the rest of the class to catch up. This form of extension, though, can be difficult to maintain if the child is especially advanced and so may not work so well for exceptionally or profoundly gifted children.

Subject matter/partial acceleration is a type of extension where a child is likely to skip to a higher level for a specific part of the curriculum. So, for example, they could be in grade 4 but attend grade 5 for literacy either by physically going into the higher classroom during the lesson, or by doing the grade 5 work in their grade 4 classroom.

Compacting and telescoping curriculum are similar types of extension but do have subtle differences. Compacting curriculum is where a student has less practice and fewer activities than a neurotypical student but completes the same work. This can be especially useful as gifted children often struggle with repetition if they get a concept early on. The time saved can then be used for other types of extension. Telescoping curriculum, however, is completing a curriculum programme in less time than is normal – so an entire grade in a semester or high school in three years instead of four.

Mentoring can be used as a type of extension where the gifted child works on more advanced work or concepts with the mentor.

Extracurricular programmes can also be used to extend a child, either by providing instruction and opportunities in entirely new areas, or by taking concepts already being learned and extending these to another level.

Concurrent/dual enrolment can be used as a form of extension/acceleration when a child is outgrowing the education the current school can provide. For example, a child in year 5 working two years above their grade level in mathematics, may find the school not so able to cater for them if they are a K–6/primary school; in this situation, it may be possible for a child to attend the local high/secondary school for maths or complete high school maths within their primary school but receive high school credit for it. Likewise, a child nearing the end of high school may be able to attend college/sixth form or receive college credit for work completed at that level. However, this particular form of acceleration can present practical difficulties in so far as it might be logistically problematic to arrange if the schools are not close together. Another consideration is uniform requirements: different schools are likely to have different uniforms and, depending on the child, they could feel isolated if not in the same uniform but changing clothes is another added dimension to consider.

Acceleration in college is where the student takes more courses and therefore extends the breadth of their study.

Extension can be a very useful form of acceleration, particularly where a child may not be socially ready to grade skip or is especially asynchronous in development and may need to be taught at several different grade levels depending on the subject. However, there are practical aspects to consider when determining if this is the right way forward for your child. Many of the types of extension discussed above focus only on a part of the school day, and gifted children are not just gifted for part of a day. It may be difficult for your child to slot back into the normal curriculum and routine after these extension periods without feeling bored or disengaged. Whether or not this is an issue will depend on your child, their level of giftedness and any asynchronous development.

Grouping

Grouping, or combined classes, can also be used to support gifted children and looks to place a child into an appropriate class either for their entire school day or for part of it. For example, dual year groups in one class – so a combined year 1/year 2 class taught by a single teacher. The advantage of this is that the children in the younger cohort get exposure to older children and also direct access to more advanced work. A child could be in year 1 officially but be taught the year 2 literacy if that is more appropriate, without needing to be moved or specially catered for outside of the composite class. However, this approach is only likely to be effective for gifted children when they are in the younger of the combined classes.

Another alternative way of grouping is streaming, which could be within a year group or across a few year groups; for example, a school could have three maths levels within a single year with students allocated dependent on their ability, or the school could combine maths for upper primary for example, and mix and stream years 4, 5 and 6, according to ability. This approach can be effective but often depends on the size of the school; it generally works better in larger schools and it also is not a method often implemented in the early years of school.

Gifted and Talented Education Programmes (GATE)

GATE programmes can be called various things depending on the school and country but all have one thing in common: they are designed to identify and group the brightest students for a particular subject. These programmes often require entry by examination and take varying forms. Some will be fairly comprehensive and cover a large part of a child's education, whereas some may only be an hour or two a week. The success of GATE programmes in the education of gifted children really depends on the type of programme and the child. A gifted child is gifted all the time, not just for a couple of hours a week. However, if the child is asynchronous in development then a few hours of extension in a particular subject may be sufficient. The other point to note is that GATE programmes are far less prevalent in primary education and often do not exist in lower primary at all.

Home schooling

Depending on where in the world you live, home schooling could be a good option for a gifted child. Each country has its own rules on home schooling and the conditions that need to be met. However, in general, home schooling allows a child to move at their own pace rather than the pace of a standard classroom. It can be highly effective as it can essentially allow a tailored curriculum but it is labour intensive and can be costly if tutors are employed. There is also no inbuilt social environment as there is in a mainstream school so this also needs to be catered for. There are many factors to consider when home schooling and if it is an option you want to look at, have a look and see if you can find home school support groups near you. These groups will help you to navigate the specific regulatory requirements of your country/state and will also provide you with ideas and groups to provide the social aspect of schooling. It is also worth considering that some countries have different exams that can be taken by home-schooled children in the last years of school and not all of these may be recognised by colleges and universities. So, it is worth checking to make sure that your child will be eligible to sit the exams required for whatever next stage they want to pursue – university entry/apprenticeships, etc.

Dedicated gifted schools

If there is a dedicated gifted school near you then this is a great option as they fully understand the specific needs of gifted children and are designed to cater for them.

This can take varying forms and usually embrace all the different types of acceleration previously discussed. They are usually more flexible in their approach to class placement than standard schools and look at each child's placement based on their current needs. Gifted schools have different requirements for entry; some will require an entrance exam and some will require a professionally administered IQ test. Unfortunately, not many of these schools exist and therefore you may not have this option. However, it is still worth researching where your closest gifted school may be as some of them do offer the option to do distance learning if you are not physically able to attend.

Schooling methods

Whilst all schools have to adhere to national educational policies, there are different methodologies they can employ. Two of these are specifically mentioned as possible acceleration options:

- Advanced Placement (AP)
- International Baccalaureate (IB)

Whilst primarily an American educational option, AP courses are now being offered in other schools around the world. Essentially, they are a higher level of course that is taken in high school but can be used as college credit (primarily at US colleges and universities but also in some others around the world.) The increased expectation and rigour of the course is a type of extension/acceleration. This is only applicable to high school students and does not offer a primary alternative.

The IB is a worldwide recognised programme that is designed to challenge and produce well rounded individuals. The IB addresses education as more than academic ability and seeks to go beyond that to a teach a broader range of human capabilities and responsibilities. The IB programme can be taught to all age groups from 3–19 years old although the Diploma Programme (last two years of school) is probably the most widely available option. The design of the IB programme is such that it allows for natural enquiry and extension by the students so can be a good option for gifted children. Some colleges, especially in the United States, will also give credit for IB courses taken in high school.

Grade skipping

When most people hear the term acceleration, grade skipping is what immediately comes to mind. It is a tool that can be highly efficient in providing for gifted children, but it does come with a lot of concerns. The majority of these surround the social and emotional readiness of a child to be in a class with older children. It is important to note here that there has been a significant amount of research into grade skipping and several longitudinal studies have been conducted (links to these studies are in the resources section). They have all concluded, that when used appropriately, there is no negative impact of grade skipping and in fact gifted children significantly benefit from it. It is also the cheapest and easiest form of acceleration open to schools – yet it is underutilised.

Both educators and parents have concerns surrounding the social and emotional readiness of children to be in a classroom with older peers. However, it is important to remember that gifted children are often more socially and emotionally mature than their neurotypical age peers and therefore, in many cases, can actually fit in better with the older children. Equally, it is interesting to consider that if a child showed significant musical or athletic ability, the same reluctance would not be present if it was suggested that they move into a more senior team or orchestra. The result is similar – the child in question would be with older children but their talent would be more appropriately catered for. In these situations it is accepted and frequently done, yet advanced academic ability is not looked at in the same way.

In *Gifted: A Primer for Parents and Educators*, Elissa McKay asks us to imagine if an elite sports administrator made comments such as, "It is very unfortunate that David's parents have encouraged him to develop exceptional football skills so far beyond his chronological age peer group." Or, "Just because some kids have extraordinary physical potential, it doesn't mean we can treat them any differently – that's elitist. All children are world-class Olympic athletes." Or even, "We're concerned about how much time Lauren spends on the tennis court; we're asking her to consider another hobby as it will help her become more well-rounded." These comments are ridiculous and would be unlikely to be said about children of high physical potential – yet they are repeatedly said about children of high academic potential.

The key thing when considering grade skipping is that research shows it is highly effective when used appropriately. Remember there are other types of acceleration, so how do you know if grade skipping will be right for your child and if it is being appropriately suggested?

Drs Susan Assouline and Nicolas Colangelo of the Belin-Blank Center have developed a tool which is specifically designed to assess if a grade skip is an appropriate approach for a child – the Iowa Acceleration Scale. It was initially developed in the 1990s and is currently on its thirrd edition. It is designed to assess children in grades K–8. Where this tool really comes in helpful is that it is designed to provide an objective look at the whole child; it looks at academic achievement, social and emotional indicators, family considerations (e.g. siblings in the same school) and then weights these based on research into acceleration. The result is a score which provides an indicator of whether the child is a good candidate for a grade skip. The Iowa Acceleration Scale is currently in use in the United States, Canada, Australia and New Zealand.

Hopefully, after reading this chapter you have a better understanding of what options may be available for your child, always keeping in mind that there is no one-size-fits-all approach and you will need to figure out what works for your child. In the next chapter we will look at how you can work with educators to determine the best solution for your child

---

The Integrated Acceleration System

In 2021 the Belin-Blank Center released a new Integrated Acceleration System. This is an online tool which will take in information and then produce a report on a child's readiness for acceleration. At the the time of writing, it is only able to comment on a grade skip; however, early entrance to kindergarten, subject acceleration and early entrance to college are all under development and will be released. Although it has been designed around the US education system, the Belin-Blank Center feel it should be compatible with international education systems as well.

7

Putting it into Practice – Getting the Best Fit for your Child

Now, at this point you may be thinking – but my child is happy at school, they have good friends, they make good grades, why do I need to worry about making any changes? This is a valid question – why exactly is appropriate school placement so important?

For some of you, it will be an obvious decision. If your child is unchallenged, unhappy or acting out at school it could well be because they are inappropriately placed and need more extension or acceleration. If though, you are lucky enough to have a child that seems to be thriving in their current school environment, the choice is not so easy. Doing nothing is certainly a valid option here, dependent on the child. In that case, take the information in this chapter on board so you are ready if you do need to step in and advocate for your child at school. But also have a think about whether your child really is being challenged enough right now.

One of the key things that is crucial to our development is to learn how to cope with challenges and how to deal with failure and disappointment. Think for a moment about two children in a classroom – one is neurotypical, the other is gifted. The gifted child grasps all the concepts quickly and easily. They can apply the knowledge to complete their work and they get top marks in everything. Everyone comments on how smart they are and the child seems happy and content. The neurotypical child struggles with some concepts, they need additional help and it takes them a few tries to get things right. The school encourages the child and the teachers help them to see that they can try again and they feel a real sense of achievement when they finally get the concept.

As they go through school, the gifted child continues to find learning easy and excels, the neurotypical child continues to take additional time to grasp some concepts but gets there in the end. Until, one year, it could be high school, it could be university, it could be before that, when the gifted child comes across a concept they don't get first time. Since they have never failed before and never really been challenged, they haven't built the foundations they need to cope with the situation. They start to doubt themselves, to doubt whether they really are clever and smart as they have been told all their lives. They feel unable to ask for help as they have always managed before. They feel it is their fault they cannot understand this concept. This could lead to a crisis for the gifted child.

Failure, and learning how to overcome it, is a crucial tool we must learn and it is a skill that gifted children are in danger of missing out on if we don't ensure they are appropriately challenged. There is a fantastic video that shows this and the link is in the resources section.

So, it is important to consider whether your child is getting everything they need to succeed from their current school placement, even if they seem happy.

Another good way to look at why appropriate school placement is so crucial is set out in a metaphor by Stephanie Tolan. Stephanie Tolan is an author and advocate for gifted children and is a senior fellow at the Institute for Educational Advancement in California. In her metaphor, Stephanie looks at a cheetah – the fastest land animal on earth which can run at 70mph. When it is running at this speed, it is easily identifiable as no other animal runs as fast. But what about when it is chasing slow prey? It won't run at 70mph so is it still a cheetah? What about if the cheetah is in captivity and confined to a cage, it cannot run at 70mph – is it still a cheetah? Stephanie then compares the cheetah to a gifted child: if a gifted child is not given a chance to be challenged (run at 70mph) in school, if they are stuck in a classroom where everything is easy for them (confined to a cage) are they still gifted?

The answer is, of course they are, just as the cheetah is still a cheetah. But it shows that it can be difficult to identify gifted children and address their needs when they are denied the opportunity to express their true nature. Just as we might visit a zoo and struggle to identify the cheetah vs. the leopard if they are not allowed to run, so too can gifted children be overlooked if they are sitting quietly in their classroom, behaving and seemingly achieving.

Conversely sometimes, natural ability is too strong and the cheetah cannot sit quietly in the cage, but may prowl up and down and lash out at those it sees outside. Similarly, says Stephanie, a gifted child stuck in an inappropriate environment may well lash out and misbehave as they are being forced to quell their own abilities. A link to the full article outlining the metaphor can be found in the resources section.

It is also important to note that children are great at adapting. If they are stuck in an environment where they do not feel challenged, or where they are conscious that they seem different to the other children, they may well adapt and start to try to fit in. This can take many forms – a child can develop a 'school personality' where they feel unable to be themselves and instead make mistakes, don't answer questions and effectively try to blend in and not stand out. My child, when placed in an environment that did not pose sufficient challenge started to do this. He chose to give deliberately wrong answers to questions he knew and started to make deliberate mistakes in spelling, etc. These children are then masking their giftedness, which can make it more of a challenge to convince the school a change is needed as they are not top of their class.

Similarly, some children struggle with fitting in. If they are not being challenged enough, they are more than likely to be bored. In some cases, this will cause the child to act out – they could become the class clown, they could be constantly fidgety, they could become angry and struggle to cope with the pent-up energy. I have heard it said that being a gifted child in an unchallenging environment is like having to watch the airline safety video on repeat. Adults would struggle to sit still and behave if forced to do that for hours at a time and yet that is what school can be like for some gifted children. It is no wonder then that some struggle to moderate behaviour or to contain their energy. However, it is also a manifestation of giftedness that makes schools question whether a change is appropriate – the child may be seen as difficult or as having behaviour problems when, in reality, boredom could be a significant factor.

The simple fact of the matter is that giftedness presents in many different ways and to differing degrees. Gifted children therefore do not necessarily conform to a stereotype. It can pose a challenge then, to identify a gifted child. In many countries, teacher training does not cover giftedness in any detail and if you think back to the rarity of some of the levels of giftedness, a teacher may well never have come across an exceptionally or profoundly gifted child. For example, a child with an IQ of 156 is a 1 in 10,000 child. A teacher may teach 30 students a year. If they have taught for 40 years, they have potentially taught 1,200 children – they are vastly experienced, but may never have come across such a child before.

I recall talking to our psychologist after my son was tested and the way she described his needs and his abilities. It all made perfect sense. I was shocked to then go to talk to schools and find that they didn't see it like that at all. And that is a key point to remember: most schools are not specialists in gifted children. They may not be approaching things from the same degree of knowledge and understanding that you are, so be prepared to work collaboratively with them and for it to take some time. It may seem as though you are constantly battling with the school but the key here is to understand that schools are not the enemy. The school is also trying to ensure the safety, happiness and education of all their students (not just yours) and so always have to keep the bigger picture in mind. However, it is true that some schools are just not open to learning or trying to understand the needs of gifted children. If you feel your school is one of these, then looking at other options – either another school or another method of education – is probably the best thing to do. If you are just banging your head against a brick wall and getting nowhere, then take your energy elsewhere and don't waste time. But, for the most part, schools are open and do want to try to help. If you are getting time with the school and if they seem willing to consider options, then pursue them and help them to understand what your child needs.

Initial approach to the school

When you first get your child's test results, or when you move to a new school, or when you first suspect your child is gifted, you will need to discuss things with the school. If your child is already attending the school, make an appointment to see your child's teacher and perhaps ask that the principal or head of learning support or whoever your school has that you feel appropriate, be present as well.

If you are moving to a new school, then it is probably best to make an appointment to see the principal and to suggest that other teachers/support staff be brought along as deemed necessary.

Make your appointment request by email and set out why you want to talk. This is your initial discussion so don't try to demand a particular resolution or even suggest one in the inital email – just set out why have asked for a meeting and why you you need to bring this to their attention. You will have time to state your requests and suggestions at the meeting.

So, for example, you could include some of the following in the initial email:

- Your child has just been identified as gifted and you would like to discuss next steps with the school.
- Your child has been having difficulties in class and you suspect giftedness so would like to discuss it with the school.
- You are moving to a new school so would like to share your child's psychological assessment and discuss their needs.

Attach any reports you have – the psychological assessment, any academic assessment reports and any previous reports from previous schools if relevant.

By setting out in an email what you are hoping to discuss and by providing the reports in advance, you give the school the opportunity to come prepared to have a meaningful discussion. They can't be expected to help if they are given pages of documents and reports at the meeting itself – you need to give them time to prepare too.

Initial meeting with the school

At the initial meeting try to remain calm and don't go with huge expectations, especially if you have just found out that your child is gifted as it can be a very emotional and difficult time. You can feel up against the clock to get things changed and in place for your child as soon as possible. I know the feeling; I went through it and I struggled with the amount of time it took to get things to a place where everyone seemed happy.

This can also be very difficult if you are talking to the school because your child is having problems as you will have a strong desire to improve things for them as soon as you can. This is completely understandable and it is important – no one wants a child to struggle or suffer, including the school. They will try to do what is best for your child, but they may or may not agree with you on what that looks like, especially at the initial meeting.

Keeping calm is important because you can have a far more productive discussion this way. Set out the information you have about your child, bring up any issues you feel they are currently going through and ask the school what they suggest. If you do have a very strong feeling or a strong recommendation from the psychologist or an educational consultant as to what should happen, bring that up as your suggestion and ask the school for their feedback.

Be prepared that you are unlikely to get exactly what you want at the initial meeting – not because the school is being difficult or obstructive but because you may be approaching the meeting from two different angles.

At the end of the meeting, recap what you have discussed and the next actions to be taken on both sides. Follow up with an email setting the points and next steps out in writing.

The waiting period

Then comes the hard part – waiting! The school will want time to consider the information and to look at feasible options. They may also want time to conduct some tests of their own. Especially if your child has just moved to a new school, they will also want time to get to know your child.

This period of waiting can be really difficult, especially if your child is struggling or unhappy. But it is important. The school needs time to carry out their assessments and to make the best recommendations they can.

I know from personal experience just how hard it is to stay away and let the school do their job but you need to try! Make sure that you have set a time frame with the school at the initial meeting so that you know you have another assessment date. New schools often feel they need around six weeks to get to know the child properly. If you are talking to your existing school, this waiting period could be shorter while they consider options which may work.

The most important thing to remember though is that you are working with the school – they are doing their part and your role is as a parent, even if you are an educator yourself. As a parent, you know your child better than probably anyone else and the reason for doing all of this – for the testing, research, advocating for your child at school – is to ensure your child is happy and thriving. That said, although giving the school space and waiting is important, if you see your child's behaviour or emotional wellbeing materially deteriorating during this time, step in – even if you are cutting the waiting time short. A child's behaviour can deteriorate rapidly in the wrong environment and it can take far longer to get them back to a happy state than it did to deteriorate.

This is the situation I found myself in. My son had just started at a new school; the school asked for time to get to know him and as hard as I found it, I was desperately trying to give them space. But in the space of three weeks, my son changed into a completely different person. We witnessed emotional and behavioural changes and he was cloaking his natural abilities. I was shocked by how rapidly the changes had occurred and checked with quite a few people – professionals and other gifted parents – to see if this could really happen so quickly. The answer was a resounding yes. So I stepped in and went back to the school earlier than originally planned. In short, give the school space but do not override your parental instincts – if your child needs a faster resolution, step in.

Why it is likely to take some time

Psychologist's report is just one piece of the puzzle

One of the things I have learnt is that whilst the psychological assessment and the views of the psychologist are very important, they are just one part of the puzzle. A psychologist may often look at things in more black and white terms. A psychometric IQ test, by design, is a structured scientific test with rules around administering; it does not cover things like personality or emotional attributes in any detail. It is conceivable that two people can score identically on an IQ test but they could still be completely different personalities and therefore the same educational solution might not be right for both individuals. However, since a psychologist is assessing the quantifiable rather than the qualitative with an IQ test, they can, and often do, make recommendations or educational suggestions based on the FSIQ number and/or the other composite scores. Now, these suggestions are still perfectly valid but you need to consider whether they suit your child's personality. Remember, there are 20 different types of acceleration; if your psychologist has recommended acceleration, it does not have to mean grade skipping. This is where it is important to pull together other informed opinions to determine what is the best for your child; the school is one of those opinions, especially if your child has already been attending prior to being identified as gifted. Other opinions could include other specialists your child might see or educational consultants or other professionals you have asked to administer academic placement or achievement tests.

Achievement or academic ability tests

IQ tests show a child's cognitive potential but not what they are currently capable of doing academically. For a school, an IQ test can be difficult to use to place a child effectively as some children will be performing well above grade level and others will not at this stage.

Remember, a gifted child is not born knowing everything, they still need to be taught. This is where it is useful to have additional academic or achievement testing done. These tests consider what a child is actually doing now and will give a score usually in terms of age or grade level – i.e. performing at an 8 year old level or reading at a 5th grade level. This allows schools to better assess workable options for a child.

Myths and lack of understanding around acceleration

Since there is a lack of understanding around acceleration and because educators are often not taught to understand and recognise giftedness, grade skipping can and does go wrong, especially if a child is not suitable for this particular method of acceleration. Schools will often fall back on a bad experience with grade skipping as a reason why they do not want to pursue it again. But every child is different and every gifted child is different. Just because a school had a previous bad experience with acceleration, does not mean that that will be the case again; unfortunately, it can be a case of once bitten, twice shy. A school that has had a negative experience is potentially going to be more apprehensive in trying again. You will therefore need to convince them that this is a different case, a different child and explain why you feel the solution will work in this case.

Schools also look at the development of the child and the school as a whole and often cite social and emotional reasons for not wanting to grade skip a child. This is an interesting point that bears further examination. Children do show varying levels of social and emotional maturity and not all children of a certain age will be identically developed. A child entering a school with their age cohort is not usually expected to pass a social or emotional standard to gain entry. However, there is that concern and expectation over gifted children being grade skipped.

Research and longitudinal studies into gifted children who have been grade skipped have shown no adverse effects on social and emotional development (links to the studies in the resources section). In fact, gifted children often find they fit in better with older children as they have similar interests and abilities. If you think about adults, we tend to make friends based on those with similar attributes to ours – either similar sense of humour, similar interests, similar stages of life. We do not generally make friends based on how close in age we are and yet we expect our children to make friends this way.

Now, rate of development and social and emotional maturity will often mean that children do gravitate towards others of a similar age to them. However, gifted children frequently feel different and unable to connect with age peers as they are often more advanced in areas. Therefore, these children may need to look outside their age peer group to find like-minded individuals.

Schools can also be reluctant to grade skip or even subject accelerate children because they feel teachers are capable of extending children within their current classroom environment, or that the school gifted and talented programme will provide sufficient extension. Again, this can be true, depending on your child and their particular level and manifestation of giftedness. If they are mildly gifted or gifted in one specific area but working at an age level for other subjects, then this may be possible. But if your child is more gifted, especially if they are exceptionally or profoundly gifted, this probably won't be sufficient due to the level and breadth of extension they are likely to need. Gifted programmes may well be able to cater for the right level, but they are often just a few hours a week – children are not just gifted one day a week!

Schools can also be reluctant to accelerate a child as they feel they will have gaps in their learning or miss out on important developmental skills such as fine motor control (especially if grade skipping in the early years). This is true; gifted children are likely to have gaps in their learning and may well need additional help in a few areas. However, you must look at the child as a whole – do the gaps prevent them from succeeding at the next level? If not, then they shouldn't be held back because of it. Some neurotypical children may have gaps at the end of an academic year but they are not held back in most cases, just given support to close the gaps.

A gifted child will usually master concepts quickly as well and therefore can efficiently close the gaps if given the right tools. One good analogy is that learning is like lace: there may be gaps in knowledge but as long as the overall level of structure is sufficient to support the child, then they can progress.

Disengagement on standardised tests

It is fairly common for gifted children to disengage if they find the task boring or unchallenging. This can pose a problem with things like standardised placement or achievement tests. These tests are often used by schools to check on the progress of students.

I have heard many instances of gifted children scoring poorly on age level tests but excelling at more advanced levels. My son is one example – he doesn't really like to read fiction books, but devours non-fiction. He was recently given two comprehension tests – he scored poorly on the test using fiction text but scored quite highly on the test using the non-fiction text, even though this was a harder level comprehension test.

What this means in practice is that, in these cases, teachers need to be willing to give gifted students harder test levels even if they don't appear to have qualified for them in order to get a true appreciation of where the child is at academically.

The second meeting

When you have your follow-up meeting with the school, once again email them beforehand with any additional reports or assessments you may have since your last appointment. Give them any new facts you feel they may need, such as changes in sleep patterns or behaviour at home.

When at the meeting, ask the school what they propose as a solution to support your child. Even if it is not what you were hoping for or expecting, try to understand their proposed solution. Ask how it's going to work. How will they support your child academically and socially? Ask them why they are not happy to give your preferred solution a try. It may be that they are struggling with a lack of understanding around some of the myths discussed throughout this and previous chapters. If that is the case and you feel strongly about your solution, share some of the facts and research but try not to bombard them with too much research.

Also, bear in mind that schools have their own cultures and personalities too. It may be that the school has decided against options for specific reasons that they cannot share with you. For example, a grade skip may not be the best course of action if the cohort of children in the receiving class is more disruptive or already includes many children in need of additional support. In such a case, the school may feel that your child will get better attention to their needs by remaining in the current class with additional support and extension. Similarly, teachers have different personalities; it could be that the school feels a particular teacher may be an especially good fit for your child (or vice versa) and may try to work out a solution to make that match. In short, schools will be assessing many different things when coming up with a proposed solution.

Try to come to an arrangement that both you and the school can support. It may be that you give the school's idea a try initially. Remember, what is decided now does not have to be the final decision; both you and the school can and should, reassess and make sure that the solution is working. In fact, it is a good idea to set a trial period for whatever solution is decided. Six weeks is a good timeframe for a trial as it gives your child and their teachers time to settle into the new routine.

At the end of the meeting, summarise the main points discussed and set out action points. Hopefully, these will include a trial period for a new solution and a few contact points within that trial period to evaluate progress and discuss any issues that may have arisen.

Follow up with an email outlining what was discussed and the decisions made.

> **Key Point to Remember**
>
> Remember, finding the right school fit is not a one-shot opportunity. Although you want to try to minimise disruption for your child, you do not have to stick with a solution, or school, if it is not working. You can make further changes if your child needs them.

What next?

If, after the trial period of the new solution, both the school and child are happy then you are probably in a good place for now. Remember that things can change though so set out times when you can reassess the situation to make sure everyone is still happy.

If, either during or at the end of the trial period, the proposed solution does not seem to be working, then you need to arrange another meeting with the school. Again, email them to explain why you want to meet and set out why you think the current arrangement is not working. Propose a new solution if you have one. At the meeting, discuss potential ways forward – changes to the current arrangement or a new option. Hopefully you will agree on the next steps and be able to set a trial period. If so, follow the steps from the previous meetings: recap your discussion and the proposed solution and set out the actions and next steps. Re-evaluate after the trial period and repeat the steps again if necessary until you get a solution that works. If at any point, you feel that you have reached the end of workable, productive discussions with the school and you still don't feel you have a solution then it may be time to re-evaluate whether this school is the right fit.

Ongoing relationship with the school

Once you have got to a place where you feel your child is happy and thriving, you need to look at maintaining the long-term relationship with the school. Many schools are excellent at maintaining a relationship with the parents and making sure they feel involved with their child's learning. Schools often use learning apps to share details of work done by your child and many schools also have open door policies for the parents to stop by and talk to the teacher before or after school. If your school has these things in place, that is great. But don't be afraid to ask if you feel you need more.

Communicate with the class teacher regularly

Check in with your child's teacher on a regular basis and bring up any changes or concerns you may have. Ask the teacher to share any concerns they might have as well. Often, by working together, you and the teacher can overcome some of the problems simply.

For example, my son's teacher noticed that he struggled to settle down to independent tasks. She brought this to my attention and I suggested using a timer as he loves to try to beat the clock. Sure enough, this helped him to focus more on the tasks at hand as he loved the idea of getting a faster time than previously. It is by no means a perfect solution but it certainly helped. By having open communication with your child's teacher, you can help by sharing some of the techniques you use at home to help your child.

Sharing research

There is a wealth of literature and research available about giftedness and it can be very tempting to want to share this with the school – just keep it in perspective! Your child's teacher has many other children to teach and care for in their classroom as well. If all the parents sent the teacher hundreds of pages of research, they would never have time to read it all! By all means share a particularly pertinent piece of research, or volunteer to share it if the teacher is interested but try not to bombard them with too much as they simply don't have the time to read it all.

Handy Hint

Keep a folder with all correspondence, test reports, scores, assessment reports and research, etc., so things are organised and easily accessible when you need them.

Get involved

If you can, get involved with the school and volunteer to help, perhaps with the parents' association or with school activities or helping in the classroom if that is welcomed. The more you get involved with the school, the more you will come to understand the ethos and culture of the school and build up good relationships.

New school year, new teachers

A new school year means new teachers and this can be a challenging time for both you and your child, especially if they have had an excellent relationship with the previous teacher. The school should pass on all the information to your child's receiving class teacher but it is worth arranging a time to meet in the first weeks of school just to say hello and address any key points you think the new teacher should be aware of.

Don't give them too much structure or expect everything to be done in exactly the same way as the previous year; different teachers have different teaching styles – and a different style may well be just as effective once you and your child get used to it. So, give the new teacher a few key points and then let them get to know your child.

If, in a few weeks or so, things don't seem to be working, go back and ask for another meeting and explain what you feel the problem is and see if you can work through it.

Set times to re-evaluate

Whilst it is important to be able to have regular contact with your child's class teacher, other people will also be involved in decisions about your child's education and it is important to arrange a time every so often – perhaps once a semester or so – to check in with everyone. This could include the principal, learning support teachers and counsellors. Arrange a time to discuss your child's progress and make sure that you are all happy that the solution you put in place is still working.

It can seem a daunting prospect to advocate for your child in a school setting. But remember, schools and educators are not the enemy and everyone wants what is best for the child. The main stumbling block usually occurs because parents and educators disagree on what is the best course of action. By remaining calm and gathering the right information, you stand a very good chance of forging a relationship of mutual respect with the school where you work together to create a solution that is right for your child.

8

The Twice-Exceptional Child

Twice-exceptional or 2e is a term often heard in the gifted community. It refers to a gifted individual that also has a second (or more) exceptionality. These exceptionalities can come in many forms and it is impossible to look at all of them in detail, so in this chapter we will look broadly at some of the key issues that can be associated with 2e as well as a few of the more common second exceptionalities.

At this point I must note that this is not a medical or psychological text and I have no first-hand experience of 2e children. The information in this chapter is purely from research and discussion with other parents and professionals who do have experience. I have included links to some more in-depth studies and reading material should you want to look deeper into any area discussed in this chapter.

Identifying a 2e Child

It can be difficult to identify a 2e child as giftedness can often mask other issues that may be present. For example, children with a learning difficulty may well be able to use their giftedness to counterbalance the learning difficulty and remain on a par with their neurotypical age-appropriate cohort. What this means is that both exceptionalities are being overlooked and this can lead to problems later on. However, it does explain why it is often difficult to attain the correct diagnosis.

There can also be situations where giftedness has already been formally identified and any further issues are attributed to that, thereby delaying identification of a second exceptionality. Or, vice versa, a diagnosis of a different exceptionality can mean that giftedness is not identified.

It is important to try to identify all the exceptionalities as each one needs to be understood and supported if your child is to thrive to the best of their ability.

IQ tests can be useful in helping to identify potential second exceptionalities. The subtests and sub-scores for the different sections of the IQ tests can illuminate weaker areas of development which could indicate a second exceptionality is present. Commonly, this manifests in lower scores in areas such as processing speed or working memory.

If your child has had a formal IQ test and the scores seem somewhat unbalanced, talk to the testing psychologist about whether or not it is worth undertaking additional tests to rule in or out a second exceptionality.

Myths surrounding 2e children

There are several common myths and misconceptions surrounding 2e children, especially regarding how they should be accommodated in schools. Here I will discuss a few of these.

Myth #1: You can't be gifted and have a learning difficulty.

This is completely false. It is absolutely possible to have both and neither is more important than the other. One of the most prevalent issues perpetuating this myth is the fact that because 2e children are both gifted and have a learning disability, neither exceptionality presents as would be expected. As mentioned above, 2e children can often mask their learning disability by using their giftedness to counterbalance it, in a way non-gifted children with learning disabilities cannot. What this means is that often these second issues can fly under the radar for a while and not be picked up until the child comes up against something for which they cannot compensate.

Myth #2: 2e children should have an education which focuses on the learning difficulty.

Both exceptionalities need to be addressed and catered to in a child's education and if this is not done, then issues can, and often do, arise. Unfortunately, as we have seen throughout the discussions in this book, gifted accommodations are not the norm. It is far more likely for a school to have a programme to accommodate and adjust for the learning difficulty. However, research has shown that only adjusting for the second exceptionality and ignoring the giftedness can have detrimental effects on a child. As we have seen, ignoring or not accommodating the giftedness can have negative consequences. The same is true if a child is 2e – all exceptionalities need to be assessed and catered to.

A 2e child should have access to the same provisions for giftedness as any other gifted child. It may be that adjustments need to be made within these provisions for the second exceptionality; but they should not be prohibited from attending gifted programmes or forms of acceleration simply because they have an additional need. The additional need should be catered to within the form of education best for the child – this means assessing and taking account of the giftedness as well.

Myth #3: 2e children are just not trying hard enough.

Unfortunately, 2e children can come up against people who feel they just simply need to try harder. When a 2e child is struggling, sometimes they are struggling in such a way that it isn't obvious to parents or teachers – especially if the giftedness has already been identified but the second exceptionality has not. People may just see a gifted child who is lazy and unmotivated, not a child who is both gifted and struggling with a second issue. This is a key reason why proper identification of all exceptionalities is crucial to providing an environment where the child can reach their full potential.

Myth #4: Behaviour issues are due to the second 'e'.

As we have discussed before throughout the book, giftedness is difficult to identify as it has no single presentation. Children who are gifted with no other exceptionality can, and often do, exhibit behavioural issues due to boredom or other factors which have nothing to do with any underlying second exceptionalities. The tendency to attribute behavioural issues to a second exceptionality can be potentially damaging. Often, it is the behavioural issues which raise a flag to potential giftedness in the first place. If the behaviour is already attributed to another exceptionality then these behavioural indicators may be overlooked and giftedness not considered. Similarly, if a child has already been identified as gifted but the gifted provision is not sufficient, attributing behavioural issues to a second exceptionality can mean this indicator is overlooked.

The roots of behavioural issues can be hard to trace, but it is important to keep an open mind and not always assume that issues are caused by one thing, particularly in the case where children are 2e.

A brief overview of some second exceptionalities

One of the difficulties in identifying some of these conditions in gifted children is that elements are often present in gifted children even when there is no other exceptionality.

For example, it is not unusual for gifted children to struggle with writing – this could be due to a second 'e' such as dyslexia or dysgraphia or it could simply be that for many gifted children, writing is a slower process than the speed at which their brain thinks of ideas and they struggle to physically keep pace with the thoughts they want to put down on paper.

One other example is organisation. Many gifted children are poor at organisation and in fact studies have shown that the part of the brain that deals with executive function is often slow to develop in gifted children (more on this point in the next chapter). This could be the explanation for poor organisational skills, but equally it could also be due to a second 'e' such as dyslexia.

Another complicating factor in identifying a second 'e' correctly is that there is a crossover in symptoms between exceptionalities and this can make it difficult to know which particular exceptionality can be causing an issue. For example, problems with writing could be caused by dysgraphia, but could also be a symptom of dyslexia. Problems with numbers and mathematical concepts could be attributed to dyscalculia but could also occur in people with dyslexia or ADHD. It is important to try to get the correct assessment as the way the second 'e' is managed could well be different.

In the sections below, I will briefly look at a few of the more common second exceptionalities:

- Dyslexia
- Dysgraphia
- Dyscalculia
- Dyspraxia
- ASD (Autism Spectrum Disorder)
- ADHD (Attention Deficit Hyperactivity Disorder)
- SPD (Sensory Processing Disorder)

This is by no means an exhaustive list and is also just a very brief overview of each exceptionality discussed. If you feel you would like more information on any of the exceptionalities outlined below, information on where to find more detail is available in the resource section.

Dyslexia – primarily affects reading and writing skills but can also affect ability to recall words quickly or follow lists of instructions and organisational skills. People with dyslexia may not be able to connect sounds with letters and may see words moving around on the page making it difficult to read. They may also have trouble with accurate spelling and be slow to write.

Dysgraphia – affects the ability to write. This can affect spelling, grammar, word size and placement as well as difficulties in the fine motor aspects of writing – e.g. holding a pencil correctly, drawing lines, etc. Dysgraphia is different to dyslexia; although dyslexics can show difficulty writing, this is usually due to a different cause than dysgraphia – for example, dyslexia can cause writing difficulties through an inability to connect words with sounds making writing slow, whereas with dysgraphia, it may be due to physical issues in fine motor control.

Dyscalculia – affects the ability to understand numbers and work with mathematical concepts. It can affect ability to understand things such as the magnitude of numbers (knowing nine is bigger than five), subitizing (being able to group objects at a glance without really counting – for example, understanding the layout of numbers on dice), telling the time and remembering number sequences like phone numbers, among other symptoms.

Dyspraxia – sometimes also known as developmental coordination disorder (DCD), affects fine and gross motor skills and coordination. Symptoms can include things like a sensitivity to loud noises, unusual posture, and difficulty in coordinating the body to perform activities such as hopping or kicking a ball.

Autism Spectrum Disorder (ASD) – according to Autism Speaks, a world-leading ASD support, awareness and research organisation, "ASD refers to a broad range of conditions characterised by challenges with social skills, repetitive behaviours and non-verbal communication." It affects how a person thinks, feels and interacts with the world around them. There is no one set of characteristics of autism, which is why it is known as Autism Spectrum Disorder. It is often possible to see signs of ASD in early childhood development – for example, no response to name, limited eye contact and late to talk. In older children, it could be characterised by an awkwardness or impairment in social interaction, a strong fixation on one or two areas of interest to the exclusion of others, repetitive behaviour and an inflexible approach to routines.

Attention Deficit Hyperactivity Disorder (ADHD) – affects behaviour and is usually characterised by impulsive behaviour and hyperactivity. There are three types of ADHD: predominantly inattentive, predominantly hyperactive and impulsive, or a combined presentation. Signs of ADHD can be present early on but it is often around the age of 6 or so that they become most apparent. Symptoms include an inability to sit still, constant fidgeting, easily distracted, trouble listening and paying attention, persistent interruptions when others are speaking, being disorganised and frequently misplacing things.

Sensory Processing Disorder (SPD) – affects how the brain processes and responds to stimuli; this can be limited to just one of the five senses or may affect some or all of them. The response can be an over- or under-reaction compared to neurotypical responses. For example, someone with SPD can be overly sensitive to light or can feel in pain if the tag of their clothes touches their skin; or they could have a high pain threshold or not respond to aural stimuli such as their name being called. Symptoms in children can include having strong reactions to light touches, lighting, food tastes or sounds, clumsiness, chewing on items like hands or clothes, not recognising when they are dirty or their nose is running.

Supporting a twice-exceptional child

Twice-exceptional children have more to deal with than neurotypical or gifted children. It is key to their well-being to try to understand and identify all the exceptionalities and to come up with a plan, both at home and school that supports the whole child. It can be difficult to identify some of the exceptionalities and there is certainly a crossover in symptoms between some of the conditions. Giftedness can also mask some of the more common symptoms and make correct identification even more of a challenge.

However, there are things you can do to help. If you believe that there is something more than just giftedness which is having an impact on your child's behaviour, talk to the experts. Assuming you are in an understanding school, talk to your child's teachers about your concerns and get their feedback. If your child sees or has seen specialists to identify giftedness, talk to them.

If you feel that things warrant further investigation, seek out a professional who can officially identify an exceptionality.

This is often a good idea even if your child seems to be functioning well and is happy as a formal diagnosis often makes it easier to access additional funding and support for your child.

Just always keep in mind that you have two (or more) challenges to juggle; try not to overlook either the giftedness or the other exceptionalities when trying to figure out the support and best educational experience for your child. You can and still should advocate for them to have their giftedness supported but there may also be further adjustments and support that need to be made within the classroom environment in order to support the other exceptionalities. Schools should make provision for this and should not stop your child from accessing the tools that they need to fulfil their potential. If you feel as though your child isn't getting the right provision, talk to your school as outlined in chapter 7 and don't be afraid to make a change.

There are lots of support groups available, both for the individual exceptionalities and for 2e children and their parents. As with gifted children, no two 2e children are exactly alike but connecting with and talking to others who face similar issues can be vastly helpful.

9

The Gifted Personality

Throughout this book we have discussed the fact that no two gifted children are alike, so how can there possibly be a gifted personality? Well, I'm using the term loosely! There are certain traits and personality features that are common in gifted children and it is these that I will discuss in this chapter. As always, the fact that your child doesn't exhibit all of these characteristics does not mean they are not gifted, just that they are their own unique individual manifestation of gifted.

However, there are likely to be at least some traits that make you go "that's my child!" By understanding where some of the behaviours of gifted children come from, we as parents are better able to create secure, safe and happy environments for our gifted children, for siblings and for the entire household.

Profiles of the gifted and talented

In 1988, psychologist Maureen Neihart and Dr George Betts created six profiles of gifted and talented learners. These profiles were one of the first attempts to make distinctions between gifted children. The profiles were designed to provide information about behaviour, emotions and needs of gifted children, but they were not meant as a diagnostic tool. However, they are useful to review, as the profiles give some suggestions for both parents and teachers in dealing with each profile type.

The profiles were reviewed and updated in 2010 and it is these revised profiles that are discussed here. The information in the profiles is fairly extensive so I will focus only on the basic overview of each profile and a short overview of the needs of that profile. There are links in the research section to the full profiles.

Type 1: The Successful

This profile is believed to account for over 90% of identified gifted and talented students. A Type 1 child is bright and motivated but often eager for teacher and parent approval rather than the full development of their potential. They have learned what works in school to achieve good grades and are usually seen as high achieving and non-problematic students who are organised and do not take risks. However, there is a danger that the child can disengage from learning and achieve these high marks with little effort, which can lead to struggles with failure later in life.

These children need to be given opportunities to be challenged, to take risks and to be independent. At school this can mean subject or whole grade acceleration and being given opportunities to develop independent learning skills as well as activities that stretch them beyond their comfort zone.

At home, parents need to give the child some independence and ability to make their own choices but also ensure they take some risks and reassure them that they do have the ability to cope with challenges, risks and failure.

Type 2: The Creative

Type 2 children are highly creative but are often not identified as gifted and therefore can feel frustration – this can manifest in impatience, anger and boredom in the classroom. These children often have high energy and can challenge rules and question the teacher. They can also show poor self-control. They are often honest, direct and have a huge amount of time for passion projects but can also have fluctuating self-esteem.

These children need to be given opportunities to connect with others and to learn strategies for coping with self-esteem and other vulnerabilities. At school this can mean allowing time for passion projects, giving direct and clear instructions, making the child aware that their feelings are ok and rewarding their creative thinking.

At home, parents can model appropriate behaviour, allow the child time to pursue interests and engage the rest of the family in these passions. Parents also need to make sure the child is aware and proud of their strengths and understands that they can talk about any psychological vulnerabilities they are feeling.

Type 3: The Underground

Type 3 children are those that perceive that they have to make a choice between peer acceptance and fulfilling their potential. Type 3 children have chosen peer acceptance. This can lead to feelings of guilt, insecurity and anxiety.

These children need to be given opportunities to connect with peers of similar abilities. They need to understand and embrace differences between people and understand that being different does not have to mean not being accepted. At school this can mean providing nurturing learning environments where children feel they can fulfil their true potential, discussing with the whole class about differences and tolerance, and allowing access to mentors. At home, parents can help by allowing the children freedom to make choices, by normalising differences and by not making comparisons to siblings.

Type 4: The At-Risk

Type 4 children are those that feel that the system has failed to meet their needs. They may be withdrawn intellectually and emotionally and feel resentment and rejection. They can be unwilling to participate in class, achieve low or inconsistent results and have low self-esteem.

These children need structure, direction and short-term goals which they feel able to achieve and that make them feel safe. At school, teachers need to make sure that they maintain their expectations of these children commensurate with their abilities and potential. They can help by providing alternative study techniques and mentorship. At home, parents can make sure their children are aware that others have confidence in their abilities, allow them to feel free to communicate issues and hold them accountable for their behaviour and work but in a way that minimises punishment.

Type 5: The Twice-Multi Exceptional

Type 5 children are 2e children who have one or more other exceptionalities in addition to being gifted. They often feel as though the focus is on the other exceptionalities and this can lead them to doubt their potential and abilities. As a result, they may be frustrated and confused, which can lead to disruptive behaviour.

These children need an environment that addresses all exceptionalities. They need to have their potential recognised and catered to, with adjustments made for any other exceptionalities. At school, this can mean addressing areas of strength and ensuring extension and acceleration in these areas with any necessary adjustments for exceptionalities. The child needs to be given opportunities to work with other gifted students and to learn to set achievable goals and to self-advocate. At home, parents can help by recognising and reaffirming the child's potential and strengths, by providing opportunities to take risks and move out of a comfort zone and by teaching the child how to recognise and set achievable goals.

Type 6: The Autonomous Learner

Type 6 students have learnt how to work effectively in school. They understand and embrace their abilities but may not hold academic achievement in the highest regard. They are tolerant of differences and have a strong sense of self. They are not afraid of failure and are willing to learn from mistakes.

These children are well-adjusted but the danger here is that parents and teachers feel they don't need a huge amount of support. In fact, these children need more support as they need to be guided and supported in facilitating new areas of growth and in increasing their independence. At school this can mean looking at a variety of acceleration options and developing a long-term learning plan, making sure the child has room for independence but also providing opportunities for mentorship and growth. At home, parents can help by providing opportunities to pursue passion projects, by allowing them a voice in family decisions and by facilitating a support network.

These profiles are not exhaustive and you may see elements of more than one in your child. However, they are a useful starting point for a discussion of personality as they do give ideas as to how to accommodate certain traits both at home and at school.

Dąbrowski's overexcitabilities

Another good avenue to explore is Kazimierz Dąbrowski's overexcitabilities. This was an eye opener for me. I was so lucky that early on in my journey as the parent of a gifted child someone pointed me in the direction of Dąbrowski. The overexcitabilities were spot on for my child and it helped me to rationalise some of the behaviours I was seeing. Once I understood these, I could find more effective ways to address the behaviours.

Kazimierz Dąbrowski was a Polish psychologist and psychiatrist. In 1964, he developed his Theory of Positive Disintegration (TPD) which included the idea of overexcitabilities (OEs). The reason OEs (as opposed to the wider TPD theory) are focused on in the discussion of giftedness is because, in an appendix to his work, Dąbrowski highlighted a study of Polish youth that was undertaken over the course of 1962. The study focused on 80 children between the ages of 8 and 23. Of these 80, 30 happened to be intellectually gifted. Dąbrowski found that every one of the gifted children exhibited at least one OE. In the years since the publication of Dąbrowski's research, several other studies have been completed considering the link between OEs and gifted children (links to some of these studies are in the resources section). The research has supported Dąbrowski's initial theory and while not all gifted children show OEs, there is far more prevalence of OEs among the gifted population than among the neurotypical population.

The Theory of Positive Disintegration

Essentially this is a theory of personality development. Dąbrowski theorised that people's personalities developed by learning to move away from social conformity to a position of self-awareness and the ability to make independent choices. In short, the ultimate goal was for a person to act based on their own determinations of right and wrong, not to follow the crowd.

The theory states five levels of development and progression is through disintegration – in essence, conflicts, changes or challenges to our beliefs. These can be positive or negative but will force a reassessment within an individual. These levels are not sequential and regression can occur, especially in cases of negative disintegration. If you are interested in learning more about TPD, there are links to further reading material and more in-depth explanations in the resources section.

So exactly what are these OEs? Dąbrowski listed five separate OEs:

- Psychomotor
- Sensual
- Intellectual
- Imaginational
- Emotional

Psychomotor overexcitability

The psychomotor OE is essentially an overdrive of the neuromuscular system. People with psychomotor OE are almost constantly moving – they may fidget and struggle with sitting still. They may talk relentlessly and sometimes rapidly and also have trouble sleeping. They often seem as though they are a bit like the Duracell Bunny – running continuously without the need to recharge their batteries!

This OE can be, and often is, misdiagnosed as ADHD due to the similarities between the physical manifestations. So, it is important to look at all the indicators to ensure you have a correct diagnosis. Psychomotor OE can be a positive thing as people with this OE can often channel the energy into a huge drive and passion for something.

Sensual overexcitability

The sensual OE refers to a heightened sensation of the five senses; this can be one or all of them and it can be both positive and negative. People with sensual OE can derive a huge amount of pleasure from tastes, sounds, smells and sights but they can also be overwhelmed by loud noises, bright lights, strong flavours, etc.

Intellectual overexcitability

The intellectual OE is characterised by a perpetually active mind. People with intellectual OE are constantly thinking and processing. They have an innate need to continually gain further knowledge. They are endlessly curious, forever problem solving and often focus on moral or ethical issues.

Metacognition (thinking about the way they are thinking) is also a key indicator of intellectual OE. People with intellectual OE will incessantly ask questions and not be satisfied with basic answers but will expect to delve into a deeper understanding. This is perhaps the most common OE found among gifted children.

Imaginational overexcitability

The imaginational OE is exactly as it sounds – a heightened imagination. People with this OE often create vivid fantasies and have imaginary friends. The OE can be so strong that it can sometimes cause a blurring of the lines between fact and fiction. Children with this OE will also sometimes have trouble focusing in class, especially on tasks which require less creativity.

Emotional overexcitability

The emotional OE is characterised by heightened emotions and feelings. These can be both positive and negative. A person with emotional OE can exhibit anxiety to the point of physical symptoms appearing, such as stomach aches, but they also have the capacity to form deep emotional relationships. They have a strong ability to feel empathy and are often very aware of their own feelings. They can experience a wave of emotions in a short space of time.

Managing OE behaviour

Now that you have an understanding of OEs, I can imagine a lot of you, as I did, are going – 'that is my child! It makes more sense now!' Understanding why your child is exhibiting certain behaviours is a great step on the path to being able to help them to deal with these OEs. It is possible that some of the behaviour you previously thought was your child acting out or being naughty is attributable to these OEs.

So now that you know about them, what can you do to try to help make home and school a happier place for you and your child? There is an element of trial and error as not all things work for all children, but I'm going to give you a few things you could try, both at home and school and just work through them and see what helps.

I have broken down the tips into the five OEs. Have a read through all of them, and even if you don't feel a particular OE is a good fit for your child, you may find that the suggestion sparks an idea for how you could adapt it to work for them.

Psychomotor OE:

- Let them fidget! Give children something to focus their fidgeting on – it could be a stress ball or an elastic band, for example. These smaller items may work well in a classroom environment as well. If, like me, you have a child that fidgets even during mealtimes, you could try using exercise bands round the legs of the chair so they can focus their energy on stretching the bands with their legs while eating.

- Give them time to use their energy. Get them to run or bike ride to and from school or, if this isn't possible, try to find time before and after school for some physical activity. In the classroom, ask the teacher if they can take short breaks at regular intervals – either for physical or for verbal exercise but mostly just a break from the task they are doing. If this isn't possible, perhaps see if they can alternate between standing and sitting at a desk in order to incorporate some movement into their tasks.

- Allow them time to be spontaneous. Give them some time to have free choice over what task to do or how to do a particular task. In school, this is often incorporated by teachers anyway and known as free time or golden time but if your school doesn't do it, or if you feel your child could benefit from additional time, talk to the teacher. It could be that 10 minutes of free time at the end of a lesson or a day are given as a reward for completing tasks, for example.

Sensual OE:

- Try to limit exposure to overstimulating environments. At home this could mean creating a calm space where colours, textures, sounds and smells are neutral and calming. At school, this could mean allowing your child to wear earplugs or headphones to block out some of the noise of the classroom or it could mean allowing them to retreat to the reading corner or other quiet classroom space for a short break if they get overwhelmed.

- Embrace the positive side of this OE. Allow your child time to explore the heightened positive sensations – listen to music, cook with them, go on a nature walk. At school, perhaps give them time to discuss or explain to the other children how they perceive music, food, textures and incorporate this into lessons as a learning experience.

Intellectual OE:

- Acknowledge the thirst for knowledge! This can be difficult if your child, like mine, is one who asks a million very detailed and difficult questions at inopportune times. But try to acknowledge their questions and get back to them later if you don't know the answers – these children usually remember a lot so try not to give them incomplete answers or answer a question you are not sure about. Show them how to find answers for themselves, either by using encyclopaedias or the internet for example. At school, ask the teacher if they can also allow time for your child to find answers to burning questions; perhaps the classroom could have a research corner set up with books and iPads if appropriate and children can ask and answer questions together.

- Give them time to work on passion projects. This is one for home and school – ask the teacher if they can have some time in the week to work on something they are keenly interested in. They could then do this at both home and school until it is finished. If the teacher agrees and wants to implement it across the whole class, the teacher could perhaps give a loose direction vaguely related to what the children are currently learning and then let the children take it from there.

- If your child is particularly focused on ethical and moral issues, show them resources where they can learn more or get involved – such as international environmental or aid organisations or, more locally, homeless shelters or soup kitchens. They could also bring this into a school environment by setting up fundraising or collecting items for recycling or charity at school if this is allowed.

Imaginational OE:

- Encourage it! Give your child opportunities to use their amazing imagination. Encourage role playing games at home or suggest they create plays or write/draw stories. At school, work with the teacher to see if there are ways that imagination can be incorporated into the task; for example, in tasks that are often not considered creative, such as maths, perhaps see if your child can spend some time creating a game that might illustrate the mathematical concept.

- Watch for the tell-tale signs that your child is caught up in their imagination. Talk to them about the fact that sometimes this is ok, and sometimes they need to focus. Come up with a signal that lets your child know that now is a time they need to be focusing. At school, share this signal with the teacher and see if they are willing to use it to keep your child focusing on the task when necessary.

- One of the negative sides of this OE can be a blurring of fact and fiction. Work with your child to allow them to gain a better understanding of this divide. Get them to place a wall mentally between the fact and fiction in their imagination. Allow them to embellish on stories or accounts of experiences but only after they have told you the factual version first. At school, you can also use this strategy and ask the teacher if they will allow your child some time to reimagine events if they have finished the task at hand. So, for example, if they are asked to write a factual account of a historical event, they must finish that accurately before being allowed to write/draw their own version.

Emotional OE:

- Accept and acknowledge the feelings. This can be difficult as often your child's reaction may seem to be an overreaction. I know from experience that it can be hard to keep perspective and not dismiss the emotion as silly, but it is important to keep in mind that it is a very real emotion for your child. Talk to your child about why they are reacting in a certain way and try to understand where the emotions are coming from. At school, explain the OE to the teacher and ask them to try to acknowledge the emotions your child displays. Perhaps ask if your child can have a quiet space to go to if they need a minute to work through an emotion.

- Try to recognise cues which provoke anxiety – this could be certain situations such as public speaking or it could be scary movies or a certain topic they come across in a book. If possible and appropriate, your child may need to avoid these situations. But this is not always appropriate or desirable and so it is also a good idea to teach them some coping mechanisms for bringing down the anxiety or emotion. For example, deep breathing or imagining yourself in your favourite spot or focusing on remembering something in order such as song lyrics or an alphabetical list. At school, talk to the teacher about which situations are especially problematic and see if these can be avoided. If not, work with the teacher to utilise the coping strategies you use at home.

- Teach your child to recognise any physical signs of an emotion – blushing, sweaty palms, shaking, stomach ache for example – and ask them to use their coping strategies when they notice these symptoms. At school, if your child is concerned about the other children's reactions, your child and their teacher could have a signal whereby if your child feels they need to leave the current situation, they could subtly let the teacher know and leave the classroom or the group temporarily.

Handy Hint

Remember not to overwhelm teachers with too many requests. They can't implement all the ideas at once, so choose the most important to focus on.

Perfectionism

Another fairly common trait in gifted children is perfectionism. There has been much research done into perfectionism in gifted children and while recent studies show that there is not necessarily a higher tendency towards perfectionism in gifted individuals, it is still an area that many gifted children struggle with. Perfectionism can range from a strong desire to do the best possible work to an anxious, neurotic approach to mistakes. Whilst some element of perfectionism could be arguably a good thing as it drives people towards producing their best effort, too much perfectionism can cause problems.

Gifted children are often used to being the best, especially if they have not been extended or accelerated in any way. It can then come as a shock if they move into a class or learn a concept that they find more challenging. They can fixate on needing to get everything perfect – it could be that a score of 9 out of 10 on a test is a cause for tears or a single spelling mistake in a piece of written work prompts a meltdown. My child has a tendency to get angry if he makes even a small mistake while writing or drawing and wants to rip up the whole thing and start again.

One of the key lessons in life is to learn to cope with failure and there are certain things you can do to try to help your child temper their tendency to perfectionism if you feel it is a little too obsessive.

- Let your child know it is ok not to be perfect all the time! As parents of gifted children, we can become so used to their high ability and achievement that we can be surprised by less than perfect work. Try to remember that there are still things that they will find more challenging and let them know it is ok not to be perfect all the time. Discuss with them how we can learn and grow through mistakes.

- Set realistic goals. Talk through tasks with your child and help them to set realistic goals. If they need to write a research paper, for example, make sure they are not trying to read all the articles Google throws up on the topic but have devised a strategy to look at which are most pertinent and how many are manageable to incorporate in the timeframe. This strategy can also work in school; perhaps the teacher can briefly have this sort of discussion with the entire class or individually with your child, just to ensure that they are not trying to achieve more than is possible.

- Have a chart tracking progress towards goals. If your child is struggling to master something, have a visual way of tracking their progress towards the goal. This way, even when they feel as though they are not getting better at it, they will have a visual reminder that they are progressing. For example, if your child is frustrated that they are not mastering times tables as quickly as they would like, have a chart that lists each individual times table and give them stickers or marks for those they have mastered. This turns a large task into smaller more manageable parts and visually demonstrates progress. This technique can also be incorporated into the classroom.

Executive function

Executive function refers to the neurological ability to organise yourself and resources to achieve a goal as well as the ability to self-regulate. Essentially it is the ability to do tasks involving organisation and planning so things like following a list of instructions or prioritising tasks to complete a goal. It begins to develop in childhood and development continues into the 20s. For many gifted children, this is one of the areas of asynchronous development and an area they often need help with.

There is some suggestion that the prefrontal cortex, which is the area of the brain used for executive function, develops slightly slower in gifted children than in neurotypical individuals. A 2006 study done by the National Institute of Mental Health studied the brain development of gifted children via MRI. It showed that the cortex layer of the brain was thinner in gifted children than neurotypical children at age 7 and it reached its thickest point in neurotypical children around age 8 or 9 but did not reach the same point in gifted children until age 12. However, once the point of thickness had been reached, the cortex matured at a faster rate in gifted children than in neurotypical children. This could well explain why gifted children struggle with executive function, particularly at a younger age as their brains are seemingly just not as developed in that area.

It may also be that the asynchronous development in executive function is explained simply by the fact that gifted children often find things easy and their brains have a unique ability to process information quickly and leap from one thing to another. This lack of challenge and the quick-thinking ability often means that gifted children don't have to use executive function skills as early on as some neurotypical age peers. For example, if a gifted child grasps a concept easily, they may not take notes on it and so do not get the development of executive function skills that the act of note taking allows.

Helping the development of executive function

It often comes as a surprise to people that a gifted individual may, for example, be amazing at manipulating large numbers in their heads but persistently forgets their homework or to put their socks on. But these sorts of behaviours can be indicative of a lack of executive function. As we get older, we are required to take more responsibility for ourselves and a lack of executive function can be especially problematic. So, how can we, as parents, help our children to develop these vital skills?

- Teach your child how to break down a task into individual steps. Work with them and ask them to explain the steps in something simple such as getting dressed or making a sandwich – for example, "I'm cutting the bread, I'm spreading the butter on, I'm adding the cheese, I'm putting the top slice on, I'm cutting the sandwich up." Whilst it may seem obvious to us, the idea of taking a task – i.e. making a sandwich – and working through what needs to be done to accomplish it can seem overwhelming to those with underdeveloped executive function.

- Play games that focus on following instructions or remembering items or patterns such as sorting games, Pictionary, Scrabble, Simon Says etc.

- Come up with ways to manage organisation and let your child know what the expectations are. It doesn't have to be elaborate; it could be as simple as a few boxes for toys and books on a shelf or it could be coloured binders and dividers for schoolwork.

- Unpack instructions and don't assume your child will understand what isn't said. For example, in my house, I'll often tell the children to put their dirty clothes in the laundry room; what I mean, of course, is to put them in the hamper but if I don't specifically say this, I get clothes thrown on the floor. My instructions weren't specific enough and my children didn't unpack the meaning and steps involved in the task. Instead, say things like "take your clothes to the laundry room and put them in the hamper."

- Use a multi-sensory approach to explanations – for example, go through your morning routine verbally with your child but also have it written down in word or picture form so they have two sensory influences to follow.

Executive function is used for many tasks at school – even from a young age, children are expected to start being organised, to take responsibility for their own school bag and belongings; to tidy away and to work on tasks independently.

A lack of executive function skills can be particularly problematic in a classroom environment as teachers do not have the time to be always helping one child with following instructions, starting tasks or remembering their belongings.

There are, however, a few tips you can implement in the classroom to help your child if they are struggling with executive function tasks:

- Create a checklist of steps that need to be done on entering the classroom, which can live in your child's schoolbag – e.g. unpack lunchbox, put away bag, sign in, hand in homework, etc. Ask the teacher if your child can have this checklist on their desk so they get used to following the steps. You could also have a second checklist for the end of the day.

- If your child's classroom doesn't have a daily schedule posted, ask the teacher if they can put one up somewhere. This breaks the day into chunks and allows a child to be reminded of what they are doing next so they can prepare.

- Ask the teacher if they can allow a few minutes at the end of class or the school day to get organised – to allow the children time to tidy away, to write down homework and to collect belongings.

- Ask the teacher if it is possible to get the children to repeat instructions with a little more detail before starting a task. So, for example, if the teacher has just read a story and has asked the class to go and write about their favourite character, ask for time where your child needs to state that they need to go to their desk, get a pen and paper and think about which character they will write about. It will allow the teacher to see that the child has actually understood the instruction and knows how to break it down into steps to begin the task.

- Ask the teacher to give time calls throughout a lesson so your child has warning of when things are to be finished/packed away.

Imposter syndrome

Imposter syndrome can affect both gifted children and their parents. Essentially it is a feeling of being a fake – feeling "I'm not that smart" or "I was just lucky, it wasn't skill". Most people, gifted or neurotypical, will experience feelings like this at some point. Asynchronous development in gifted children can heighten these feelings.

I know a lot of parents, myself included, idly wonder sometimes about whether the IQ test scores could possibly be right when we see our apparently gifted child playing the fool or hitting their sibling. But remember, gifted children are still children and will still behave like children at times!

However, imposter syndrome can be more damaging than just an idle thought. For children who begin to doubt their abilities, it can have an impact on their self-esteem and confidence.

Imposter syndrome can occur for many reasons; a lack of executive function skills, for example, can make a child feel inadequate and doubt themselves in certain situations. Or, if a gifted child comes up against a concept they find hard to grasp after years of things coming easily, it can be a severe blow to self-confidence. Imposter syndrome can manifest in different ways; a child could be angry or anxious or suddenly stop doing things they used to love. If you find yourself in this situation and your child is doubting themselves, there are things you can do to help your child:

- Provide encouragement. Remind them they can do this and let them know it's ok to make mistakes and that trying is a part of learning.

- Praise the achievements in a piece of work. Often a child will feel their entire work is inadequate from one mistake – focus on the positives and praise them.

- Keep reminders of their achievements so that when they are feeling down, you can show them that they are capable and can achieve.

- Find someone they can connect with. If possible, an older child or teen who can fulfil a mentoring role. Hearing from others that these feelings are normal can help a child realise they are not alone.

Sleep and the gifted child

Sleep can be a challenge for gifted children. There is research to suggest that gifted children need less sleep – we know their brains have physical differences so it isn't really a stretch to assume that needing less sleep could be part of this.

Many parents of gifted children struggle with the sleep patterns of their kids. After an exhausting day spent answering endless questions to satisfy their curiosity or keeping up with their boundless energy, as parents we want (and deserve!) some quiet adult time. But, if your experience is anything like mine, that longed-for quiet time becomes hours of trekking up and down stairs trying to get your child to go to sleep!

Although there is no magic solution for the sleep issue, there are a few things you can try to help your gifted child get to sleep. But, before we look at those, let's discuss why sleep is so elusive for gifted children in the first place.

- Their brain just won't shut off. Gifted children, as we know, are often highly curious and continuously seek knowledge about how the world around them works. When they go to bed, free of other distractions, their brains often go into overdrive and come up with all sorts of questions they need answers to.

- They need longer than average to wind down to a sleepy state. Gifted children are often very energetic, very curious and seemingly always on the go. When they go to bed, we are asking them to go from running at 100mph to 0 just like that and they often can't. They need time to slow down, to process the day and to wind themselves down to sleep.

- They just aren't tired! Gifted children often need less sleep, so if you are putting your 6-year-old gifted child to bed at the same time as other neurotypical 6-year-olds, they just may not be tired yet. However, it is important to make sure they are getting enough sleep – if they aren't sleeping much but are alert, energetic and functioning then the amount of sleep is probably sufficient. If, on the other hand, they are irritable, sluggish and struggling to focus, then they likely need more sleep.

So, what can we do to help these children get the sleep they need and for us parents to get some well-deserved quiet time? First, try to determine why your child isn't sleeping. Is it due to not being tired or needing time to wind down? Once you have a better understanding of why, it can help you to form a workable solution. As with everything, different things can work for different children but here are a few things to try:

- Don't focus on falling asleep – as you must know from sleepless nights, lying in bed willing ourselves to go to sleep never seems to work. So, we can't expect a gifted child to sleep just because we tell them to. Instead set boundaries, i.e. now is quiet time, you have to stay in your bed and you can only do quiet activities such as reading. By putting less stress on actually falling asleep, they are more likely to relax and then, hopefully, fall asleep!

- Give them some quiet alone time before bed – this can be in their bedroom or another quiet space (especially if they share a bedroom) but allow them time to start winding down and processing the day so they don't have to do this at bedtime.

- Give them a calm sensory space – this is particularly useful for children who have sensory sensitivities or a second exceptionality such as SPD. Ensure their bed is free of sensory distractions – no itchy labels in pyjamas or scratchy bedcovers. You could also try weighted blankets or look at getting a bed canopy to give your child a safe cocoon-like environment free of distractions.

- Go through a bedtime routine that involves turning the brain off – this could be through breathing exercises, meditation or even something as simple as flicking a switch and getting your child to imagine they are really turning their brain off.

- Give them something else to focus on – this could be music or an audiobook, for example. This allows the child to be lying down in bed, hopefully with their eyes closed but it gives their brain a distraction to focus on instead of coming up with more questions! Audiobooks can be a very useful tool for younger gifted kids who can't read yet as it gives them a peaceful "activity" to occupy their brain, much as older children may do with reading to calm down.

With luck, some of these tips will work for your child and help them to get the rest they need. But, if they don't work, many parents have had success with melatonin supplements as an aid to help the sleep of their gifted children, although this should only be given after a discussion with a doctor.

As you can see from the discussions above, gifted children face challenges and exhibit behaviours that may require some adaptation in parenting and teaching in order to achieve the best outcome. I hope the information above has helped you to understand some of the personality traits and behaviours you may have been seeing in your child and that some of the suggestions will work for you. Remember that parenting a gifted child is an ongoing process and you may need to revisit this chapter several times to try new ideas as your child grows.

Conclusion

Parenting a gifted child is a journey. It is one that will have ups and downs but one that can be incredibly fulfilling. A gifted child will face many of the same challenges involved in growing up as their neurotypical peers, but there are also unique challenges which need to be understood and addressed in order to make sure your child is happy and thriving.

Hopefully, having read through this book, you have a better understanding of the somewhat nebulous concept of giftedness. It can be difficult to know what to do and where to turn when you see your child struggling, especially given a general lack of understanding around the concept, that each gifted child is an individual and that there is no one set of criteria, which makes the challenge even more difficult.

But you are not alone, even if at times it may feel like it. There are many other parents and children out there with similar experiences. Find the support groups and use them, especially when you need a bit of a reality check or a reassurance that things are going to be ok.

CONCLUSION

Keep track of the end goal – a happy, thriving child – and remember that what works now, may not work in the future but that you have the tools and knowledge to help facilitate whatever changes your child may need.

Work with your school and keep an open line of communication with your child's teachers. Try to develop a working relationship that supports your child and reinforces routines, concepts and behaviour management techniques at home and at school, but do not be afraid to change if your situation warrants it.

Don't be afraid of trial and error. Try something – a skill, a schooling method, a behaviour technique – but if it doesn't work, try something else. The decisions you make now don't have to be the final ones; you can make changes if they are needed. And always remember that each gifted child is unique – just because something worked for one parent and child, doesn't mean it will work for you and that's ok! You will find what does work for you and your family.

Keep this book close, especially if you have more than one child as research suggests siblings are usually within 10 IQ points of each other. If you have younger children, you may be about to begin this journey all over again and there is no doubt it will be a different one!

Finally, over the page is a quick recap of some of the most important points we have covered in this book. Come back to this list whenever you need a quick reminder.

Key Points to Remember

- Children are not just gifted one day a week – they are gifted all the time.

- There is a physical difference in the brains of gifted people compared to neurotypical brains.

- Giftedness is not the same as academic achievement. The two often go together, but not always.

- Gifted children often develop asynchronously.

- Giftedness comes in degrees and the degree of giftedness usually correlates to the amount of adjustment needed.

- There is no one-size-fits-all approach to giftedness – each child is unique.

- There is likely to be no perfect solution but options that may be better than the current situation.

- There is a general lack of understanding around giftedness – acknowledge this and collaborate to find a solution.

Glossary

Acceleration: Moving through the school curriculum at a faster rate than is typical. Twenty different types of acceleration have been identified.

ADHD: Attention Deficit Hyperactivity Disorder – a chronic neurodevelopmental disorder usually diagnosed in childhood, characterised by inattentiveness, hyperactivity and impulsiveness.

ASD: Autism Spectrum Disorder – a complex developmental disorder which can lead to challenges in social interaction and communication as well as repetitive behaviours.

Asynchronous development: an uneven rate of development in one or more of the following areas: cognitive, emotional, social and physical. Often a trait found in gifted individuals.

Bell curve: A graph depicting a normal distribution shaped like a bell with a larger central peak tapering at each end. It depicts normal distribution which is a distribution that occurs naturally in many situations.

Cognitive potential: The ability to acquire brain-based skills needed to understand tasks such as acquiring knowledge and reasoning. Cognitive skills are the mechanism or building blocks of how a person learns.

Dyscalculia: A condition which affects the learning and comprehension of arithmetic and number skills.

Dysgraphia: A neurological disorder which affects the ability to write.

Dyslexia: A neurological disorder which affects the ability to identify speech sounds and understand how these sounds relate to letters and words.

Dyspraxia: A developmental brain condition which affects fine and gross motor skills, coordination and motor planning.

FSIQ: Full Scale Intelligence Quotient (Full Scale IQ). An individual's complete cognitive capacity.

Gagné's Differentiated Model of Giftedness and Talent: A psychological model differentiating between natural abilities (giftedness) and acquired abilities (talent).

GATE: Gifted and Talented Education – can refer to specific policies or programmes within a school or education system.

Gifted: The cognitive potential and natural ability which places an individual in the top 10% of the population. It can be characterised with asynchronous development and does not always translate potential into achievement.

IQ test: Intelligence Quotient test – a standardised test which assesses cognitive ability.

Neurotypical: An individual who has developed typically in areas including developmental, cognitive and intellectual abilities.

Renzulli's Three Ring Model of Giftedness: A psychological model which proposes that in order for giftedness to translate to actual behaviour then three factors need to be present: above average ability, creativity and task commitment.

SPD: Sensory Processing Disorder – a neurological condition which affects the brain's ability to process information relating to the five senses.

Standard deviation: A measurement of how far away from the average of the group a number or entry is. The lower the standard deviation number, the closer to the average.

Twice exceptional: Refers to a gifted individual who also has one or more secondary conditions.

Working memory: allows the brain to store information temporarily until it is needed. It allows the brain to keep hold of information while not losing track of what is being done at the time.

2e: A common abbreviation for twice-exceptional.

Resources

General Resources:

The Gifted Development Center: https://www.gifteddevelopment.org/

The National Association for Gifted Children: https://www.nagc.org

The Daimon Institute: https://www.daimoninstitute.com/

The Davidson Institute: https://www.davidsongifted.org/

The Acceleration Institute at the Belin-Blank Center: http://www.accelerationinstitute.org/

SENG – Supporting the Emotional Needs of the Gifted. https://www.sengifted.org/

Hoagies Gifted: https://www.hoagiesgifted.org/

Chapter 1:

Defining Giftedness

"Defining Gifted." Institute for Educational Advancement. https://educationaladvancement.org/what-is-gifted/

"What is Giftedness?" National Association for Gifted Children. https://www.nagc.org/resources-publications/resources/what-giftedness

Neurological Research

Sousa, David A. (2009). "What is a Gifted Brain?" in Sousa, David A. *How the Gifted Brain Learns.* Sage Publishing. https://www.sagepub.com/sites/default/files/upm-binaries/32712_Sousa_(Gifted_Brain)__Ch1.pdf

"Giftedness and the Brain." *The Psychologist* (June 2009). https://thepsychologist.bps.org.uk/volume-22/edition-6/giftedness-and-brain.

"How Gifted Brains Function and Learn." Oak Crest Academy (Sept 2017). https://oakcrestacademy.org/how-gifted-brains-function/

Tetreault, Nicole A. and Zekreski, Matthew J. "The Gifted Brain Revealed Unraveling the Neuroscience of the Bright Experience." *GHF Dialogue.* https://ghfdialogue.org/the-gifted-brain-revealed-unraveling-the-neuroscience-of-the-bright-experience/

Fisher, Tamara. (2010). "What Brain Imaging shows Us About Gifted Learners." *EdWeek*. https://www.edweek.org/education/opinion-what-brain-imaging-shows-us-about-gifted-learners/2010/02

Singer, Emily. (2006). "Why Some Kids Are Smarter." *MIT Technology Review*. https://www.technologyreview.com/2006/03/30/229362/why-some-kids-are-smarter/

Theoretical Frameworks of Giftedness

"Theoretical Frameworks for Giftedness." National Association for Gifted Children. https://www.nagc.org/theoretical-frameworks-giftedness

"Gagné's Differentiated Model of Giftedness and Talent." *Journal for the Education of the Gifted*. Vol. 22 No. 2 pp.230-234 Jan 1999. https://journals.sagepub.com/doi/10.1177/016235329902200209

Renzulli, Joseph & Piaget, Jean. (2005). "The Three-Ring Conception of Giftedness: A Developmental Model for Promoting Creative Productivity." In *Conceptions of Giftedness*. https://www.researchgate.net/publication/237668711_The_Three-Ring_Conception_of_Giftedness_A_Developmental_Model_For_Promoting_Creative_Productivity

Renzulli, J. (1999) "What is this thing called giftedness, and how do we develop it? A twenty-five-year perspective." Renzulli Center for Creativity, Gifted Education and Talent Development. https://gifted.uconn.edu/schoolwide-enrichment-model/what_is_giftedness/

"Schoolwide Enrichment Model." Renzulli Center for Creativity, Gifted Education and Talent Development. https://gifted.uconn.edu/schoolwide-enrichment-model/

Traits of Gifted Children

"Traits of Giftedness." National Association for Gifted Children. https://www.nagc.org/resources-publications/resources/my-child-gifted/common-characteristics-gifted-individuals/traits

Correll, Robyn (2019). "12 Signs of a Gifted Child." https://www.care.com/c/stories/3409/20-top-traits-of-gifted-children/

Palmer, David (2011). "Is Your Child Gifted? What to Look For, Why You Should Know." *Psychology Today*. https://www.psychologytoday.com/gb/blog/gifted-kids/201105/is-your-child-gifted-what-look-why-you-should-know

Chapter 2:

Heredity and Giftedness

Snyderman, Mark P. and S. Rothman. "Survey of Expert Opinion on Intelligence and Aptitude Testing." *American Psychologist* 42 (1987): 137-144. http://lepo.it.da.ut.ee/~spihlap/snyderman%40rothman.pdf

Plomin, R. (1999). "Genetics and intelligence." In N. Colangelo & S. G. Assouline (eds.), *Talent development III: Proceedings from the 1995 Henry B. and Jocelyn Wallace National Research Symposium on Talent Development* (pp. 19–39). Scottsdale, AZ: Gifted Potential Press.

IQ Tests

McGrath M.C. (2011). "Deviation IQ." In Goldstein S., Naglieri J.A. (eds) *Encyclopedia of Child Behavior and Development.* Springer, Boston, MA. https://doi.org/10.1007/978-0-387-79061-9_838

Cherry, Kendra (2020). "How Average IQ Scores are Measured." https://www.verywellmind.com/what-is-the-average-iq-2795284

"IQ and Educational Needs." The Davidson Institute. https://www.davidsongifted.org/search-database/entry/a10877

"Measuring Intelligence." Lumen: Boundless Psychology. https://courses.lumenlearning.com/boundless-psychology/chapter/measuring-intelligence/

Stevens, Alison Pearce (2016). "What is IQ and How Much Does It Matter?" Science News for Students. https://www.sciencenewsforstudents.org/article/what-iq-and-how-much-does-it-matter

Flynn Effect

"Flynn Effect." Good Therapy. https://www.goodtherapy.org/blog/psychpedia/flynn-effect

Trahan, Lisa H et al. "The Flynn effect: a meta-analysis." *Psychological Bulletin* vol. 140,5 (2014): 1332-60. https://www.ncbi.nlm.nih.gov/pmc/articles/PMC4152423/

Chapter 3:

Stanford-Binet

"Stanford-Binet Subtests." https://stanfordbinettest.com/all-about-stanford-binet-test/stanford-binet-subtests

Roid, Gale, H. (2016). "Stanford-Binet Intelligence Scales Fifth Edition Online Scoring and Report System User Guide." https://www.proedinc.com/Downloads/14462%20SB-5_OSRS_UserGuide.pdf

"Stanford-Binet Intelligence Scale." *Science Direct.* https://www.sciencedirect.com/topics/medicine-and-dentistry/stanford-binet-intelligence-scale

Cherry, Kendra (2020). "Alfred Binet and the Simon-Binet Intelligence Scale." https://www.verywellmind.com/alfred-binet-biography-2795503

WISC

Kimbell, Anne-Marie (2015). "An Overview of the WISC-V." https://nspa.wildapricot.org/resources/Documents/kimbell__wisc-v_nspa_handout.pdf

"Weschler Intelligence Scale for Children (WISC V)." Child and Educational Psychologist. https://www.child-psychologist.com.au/wechsler-intelligence-scale-for-children.html

WPPSI

"WPPSI-IV." South County Child and Family Consultants. https://southcountychildandfamily.com/wppsi-iv/

"The Boldly Reimagined WPPSI-IV." Pearson. http://images.pearsonclinical.com/images/Products/WPPSI-IV/brochure.pdf

"WPPSI-IV: Frequently Asked Questions." Pearson. https://www.pearsonclinical.com.au/files/WPPSI-IV%20FAQ.pdf

"What is the WPPSI and What Does It Measure?" Washington International School. https://www.wis.edu/uploaded/Admissions/What_Is_The_WPPSI_and_What_Does_it_Measure.pdf

Woodcock-Johnson

Decker, S. L. et al. (2016). *Assessment of Executive Functions using the Woodcock Johnson IV Test of Cognitive Abilities.* (Woodcock Johnson IV Assessment Service Bulletin No. 9). Itasca, IL: Houghton, Mifflin Harcourt. https://www.hmhco.com/~/media/sites/home/hmh-assessments/clinical/woodcock-johnson/pdf/wjiv/wjiv_asb_9.pdf?la=en

Schrank, Fredrick A. (2014). "Introducing the Woodcock-Johnson IV." https://www.hmhco.com/~/media/sites/home/hmh-assessments/clinical/woodcock-johnson/pdf/wjiv/wj_iv_author_newsletter_winter_2014.pdf?la=en

General

Rapp, Rhonda. "What Tests Assess." https://higherlogicdownload.s3.amazonaws.com/AHEAD/38b602f4-ec53-451c-9be0-5c0bf5d27c0a/UploadedImages/SIGS/LD_-_ADHD/What_Tests_Assess_--_by_Dr__Rhonda_Rapp.pdf?fbclid=IwAR135Iz5kdex7hLPCtkB5ymPpVce-r9WSOg5t3B-qY6ngMaocpJmbDHATpU

"Description of Cognitive Subtests." https://individualizedassessment.files.wordpress.com/2017/09/cognitive-subtest-descriptions.pdf

Chapter 4:

IQ Rarity

"IQ Percentile and Rarity Chart." IQ Comparison Site. https://www.iqcomparisonsite.com/iqtable.aspx

Ruf's Levels of Giftedness

Ruf, Deborah (2007). "Tips for Parents: How Level of Giftedness, Gender and Personality Affect School Behaviour and Learning." The Davidson Institute. https://www.davidsongifted.org/search-database/entry/a10480

Ruf, Deborah L. (2019). "Ruf Estimates of Levels of Giftedness." https://deborahruf.medium.com/ruf-estimates-of-levels-of-giftedness-7213a77089e9

Munson, Eleanor (2011). "The Five Levels of Giftedness." Dallas Educational Consultants. https://eleanormunsonphd.com/2011/01/the-five-levels-of-giftedness/

Chapter 5:

Global Gifted Groups

USA: Davidson Young Scholars: https://www.davidson-gifted.org/young-scholars

UK: Potential Plus: https://potentialplusuk.org/

Hong Kong: Hong Kong Academy for Gifted Education: https://www.hkage.org.hk/

Australia: Australian Association for the Education of the Gifted and Talented: http://www.aaegt.net.au/

New Zealand: New Zealand Association of Gifted Children: https://www.giftedchildren.org.nz/

South Africa: Gifted Children South Africa: https://www.giftedchildrensa.co.za/

Social and Emotional Factors: Friendship

Gross, Miraca. (2002). "'Play Partner' or 'Sure Shelter': What Gifted Children Look for in Friendship." Seng Newsletter. https://www.sengifted.org/post/play-partner-or-sure-shelter-what-gifted-children-look-for-in-friendship

Chapter 6:

Acceleration and Schooling Research

Colangelo, N et al. (2004). *A Nation Deceived: How Schools Hold Back America's Brightest Students.* The Templeton National Report on Acceleration. Connie Belin & Jacqueline N. Blank International Center for Gifted Education and Talent Development, University of Iowa. http://www.accelerationinstitute.org/nation_deceived/

Gross, Miraca. (2006). "Exceptionally Gifted Children: Long-Term Outcomes of Academic Acceleration." *Journal for the Education of the Gifted.* Vol. 29. https://doi.org/10.4219/jeg-2006-247

Assouline, S et al. (2015). *A Nation Empowered. Evidence Trumps Excuses Holding Back America's Brightest Students.* Connie Belin & Jacqueline N. Blank International Center for Gifted Education and Talent Development, University of Iowa. http://www.accelerationinstitute.org/Nation_Empowered/

Gross, Miraca. "Radical Acceleration of Highly Gifted Children: An annotated bibliography of international research on highly gifted young people who graduate from high school three or more years early." http://docplayer.net/6920885-Radical-acceleration-of-highly-gifted-children.html

Chapter 7:

Learning to deal with challenges

Video - "James and Susie." Northwest Gifted Child Association. 2015. https://www.youtube.com/watch?v=IIrvZ4fwBKU

Tolan, Stephanie. (1996). "Is It a Cheetah?" http://www.stephanietolan.com/is_it_a_cheetah.htm

Social Emotional Studies

Shaughnessy, Michael. (2019). "9 Important Topics about the Social and Emotional Needs of the Gifted. (An Interview.)" SENG. https://www.sengifted.org/post/9-important-topics-about-the-social-and-emotional-needs-of-the-gifted-an-interview

Neihart, M. "The Social and Emotional Needs of Gifted Children: What Do We Know?" National Institute of Education. https://www.nagc.org/sites/default/files/WebinarPowerPoints/The%20Social%20and%20Emotional%20Development%20of%20Gifted%20Children%20with%20Assessing%20Services.pdf

Gross, M. (1993). "Factors in the Social Adjustment and Social Acceptability of Extremely Gifted Children." In N. Colangelo & S. G. Assouline (eds.), *Talent development II: Proceedings from the 1993 Henry B. and Jocelyn Wallace National Research Symposium on Talent Development* (pp. 19–39). Great Potential Press Inc.

Field, T. et al. (1998). "Feelings and Attitudes of Gifted Students." *Adolescence.* Vol. 33 No. 130. https://miami.pure.elsevier.com/en/publications/feelings-and-attitudes-of-gifted-students

Gross, M. (1989). "The Pursuit of Excellence or the Search for Intimacy? The Forced-Choice Dilemma of Gifted Youth." *Roeper Review.* Vol. 11 No. 4. https://doi.org/10.1080/02783198909553207

Chapter 8:

2e Research

Arky, Beth. "Twice-Exceptional Kids: Both Gifted and Challenged." Child Mind Institute. https://childmind.org/article/twice-exceptional-kids-both-gifted-and-challenged/

Perler, Seth. "Is My Child Twice Exceptional or 2e? [The Ultimate Guide.]" https://sethperler.com/child-2e-twice-exceptional-ultimate-guide/

"Twice-Exceptional Students." National Association for Gifted Children. https://www.nagc.org/resources-publications/resources-parents/twice-exceptional-students

Myths surrounding 2e

Morin, Amanda. "7 Myths About Twice-Exceptional (2E) Students." Understood. https://www.understood.org/en/friends-feelings/empowering-your-child/building-on-strengths/7-myths-about-twice-exceptional-2e-students

Taylor, L and Van Hoekelen, S. "Myths About 2e Students." https://simplebooklet.com/mythsof2estudents#page=0

Postma, Michael. "The 2e Student Damaging Myths." SENG Europe. https://sengifted.eu/the-2e-student-damaging-myths/

Dyslexia

"About Dyslexia." British Dyslexia Association. https://www.bdadyslexia.org.uk/dyslexia/about-dyslexia/what-is-dyslexia

"Test for Dyslexia. 37 Common Traits." Davis Dyslexia Association International. https://www.dyslexia.com/about-dyslexia/signs-of-dyslexia/test-for-dyslexia-37-signs/

"What is Dyslexia." Australian Dyslexia Association. https://dyslexiaassociation.org.au/what-is-dyslexia/

Dysgraphia

"Warning Signs of Dysgraphia." Health Prep. https://healthprep.com/mental-health/signs-of-dysgraphia/

"Understanding Dysgraphia." International Dyslexia Association. https://dyslexiaida.org/understanding-dysgraphia/

Eckerd, Marcia. "Dysgraphia: An Overview." Smart Kids with Learning Disabilities. https://www.smartkidswithld.org/first-steps/what-are-learning-disabilities/dysgraphia-an-overview/

"Dysgraphia: What You Need to Know." Understood. https://www.understood.org/en/learning-thinking-differences/child-learning-disabilities/dysgraphia/understanding-dysgraphia

Dyscalculia

Jacobson, Rae. "How to Spot Dyscalculia." Child Mind Institute. https://childmind.org/article/how-to-spot-dyscalculia/

"What is Dyscalculia." Dyslexia-SPELD Foundation. https://dsf.net.au/learning-difficulties/dyscalculia/what-is-dyscalculia

Frye, Devon. (2020). "What is Dyscalculia? Math Learning Disability Overview." *ADDitude: Inside the ADHD Mind.* https://www.additudemag.com/what-is-dyscalculia-overview-and-symptom-breakdown/

Rosen, Peg. "The Difference between Dyslexia and Dyscalculia." Understood. https://www.understood.org/en/learning-thinking-differences/child-learning-disabilities/dyslexia/the-difference-between-dyslexia-and-dyscalculia

Dyspraxia

"Dyspraxia at a Glance: What is Dyspraxia?" Dyspraxia Foundation. https://dyspraxiafoundation.org.uk/about-dyspraxia/dyspraxia-glance/

"Dyspraxia Facts." Dyspraxia Foundation USA. https://dyspraxiausa.org/symptoms/dyspraxia-facts/

"How Dyspraxia Differs from Other Developmental Delays in Children." Healthline. https://www.healthline.com/health/dyspraxia

ADHD

"Symptoms and Diagnosis of ADHD." Centers for Disease Control and Prevention. https://www.cdc.gov/ncbddd/adhd/diagnosis.html

"About ADHD: A Guide for Children." ADHD Foundation: The Neurodiversity Charity. https://www.adhdfoundation.org.uk/wp-content/uploads/2019/01/Childrens-Guide_FINAL.pdf

"What is ADHD?" ADHD Australia. https://www.adhdaustralia.org.au/about-adhd/what-is-attention-deficit-hyperactivity-disorder-adhd/

"Everything You Need to Know About ADHD." Healthline. https://www.healthline.com/health/adhd

"What is ADHD." Understood. https://www.understood.org/en/learning-thinking-differences/child-learning-disabilities/add-adhd/what-is-adhd

ASD

"Autism Spectrum Disorder Fact Sheet." National Institute of Neurological Disorders and Stroke. https://www.ninds.nih.gov/Disorders/Patient-Caregiver-Education/Fact-Sheets/Autism-Spectrum-Disorder-Fact-Sheet

"What is Autism Spectrum Disorder?" American Psychiatric Association. https://www.psychiatry.org/patients-families/autism/what-is-autism-spectrum-disorder

"What is Autism?" Autism Spectrum Australia. https://www.autismspectrum.org.au/about-autism/what-is-autism

"About Autism." Child Autism UK. https://www.childautism.org.uk/about-autism/

SPD

"Does My Child Have a Sensory Processing Disorder?" The Sensory Seeker. https://thesensoryseeker.com/does-your-child-have-sensory-processing-disorder/

"What is SPD?" SPD Australia. https://spdaustralia.com.au/about-sensory-processing-disorder/

"Understanding Sensory Processing Disorder." STAR Institute. https://sensoryhealth.org/basic/understanding-sensory-processing-disorder

"Sensory Processing Disorder (SPD)." Kid Sense. https://childdevelopment.com.au/areas-of-concern/diagnoses/sensory-processing-disorder-spd/

Chapter 9:

Profiles of the Gifted and Talented

Betts, George & Neihart, Maureen. (1988). "Profiles of the Gifted and Talented." *Gifted Child Quarterly* 32(2) 248-253.

Betts, George and Neihart, Maureen. (2017). "Profiles of Gifted, Talented and Creative Learners." https://uncw.edu/ed/aig/documents/2017/profiles%20of%20the%20gifted%20talented%20and%20creative.pdf

Betts, George and Neihart, Maureen. (2010). "Revised Profiles of the Gifted and Talented." https://docs.google.com/viewer?a=v&pid=sites&srcid=c3Rqb3NlcGhzLmNvLm-56fHN0LWpvc2VwaC1zLWNhdGhvbGljLXNjaG9vb-C1wdWtla29oZS1nYXRlfGd4OjVkZWVkNmQ5Yjl-jMzJjYmE

"Gifted Underachievers." ACT Government: Education and Training. https://www.education.act.gov.au/__data/assets/pdf_file/0009/587304/Gifted-Underachievers.pdf?fbclid=IwAR0UNsSjuhYTq3RVFEcSSsrbGD944OI3cMcVcjsKx-K3ArXW0Yqsm9IZXlJQ

Dąbrowski – Theory of Positive Disintegration

"The Theory of Positive Disintegration." https://positivedisintegration.com/Thekeypoints.htm

Ackerman, Courtney (2020). "Theory of Positive Disintegration 101: On Becoming Your Authentic Self." *Positive Psychology.* https://positivepsychology.com/dabrowskis-positive-disintegration/

Mendaglio, Sal (2019). "Dabrowski's Theory of Positive Disintegration: Some implications for teachers of gifted students." SENG. https://www.sengifted.org/post/medaglio-dabrowski

Dąbrowski – Overexcitabilities

Mendaglio, Sal and Tillier, William. (2006). "Dabrowski's Theory of Positive Disintegration and Giftedness: Overexcitability Research Findings." *Journal for the Education of the Gifted.* Vol. 30 No. 1. https://files.eric.ed.gov/fulltext/EJ750762.pdf

Lind, Sharon. (2011). "Overexcitability and the Gifted." SENG. https://www.sengifted.org/post/overexcitability-and-the-gifted

"Overexcitabilities and Why They Matter for Gifted Kids." Raising Lifelong Learners. https://raisinglifelonglearners.com/overexcitabilities-and-why-they-matter-for-gifted-kids/

"Gifted Overexcitabilities: How Gifted Children Experience the World Differently." Soaring with Snyder. https://www.soaringwithsnyder.com/2016/01/gifted-101-overview-of.html

Perfectionism

Pyryt, M. (2007). "The Giftedness/Perfectionism Connection: Recent Research and Implications." *Gifted Education International.* Vol. 23 Issue 3. https://doi.org/10.1177/026142940702300308

Silverman, Linda Kreger. (1999). "Perfectionism." *Gifted Education International*. Vol. 13 Issue 3. https://journals.sagepub.com/doi/10.1177/026142949901300303

"Perfectionism." National Association for Gifted Children. https://www.nagc.org/resources-publications/resources-parents/social-emotional-issues/perfectionism

Post, Gail. (2018). "Abandoning Perfectionism." Gifted Challenges. https://giftedchallenges.blogspot.com/2018/11/abandoning-perfectionism.html

Executive Function

"Gifted Learners and Executive Function." National Association for Gifted Children. https://www.nagc.org/gifted-learners-and-executive-functioning

"Executive Function." (2017). Living With Geniuses." https://lwallin.wordpress.com/2017/02/01/executive-function/

Conrad, Lisa. (2019). "The Role of Executive Function in Gifted Children." Global #gtchat. https://globalgtchatpoweredbytagt.wordpress.com/2019/04/18/the-role-of-executive-function-in-gifted-children/

"Executive functioning Activities for Small Children." Raising Lifelong Learners. https://raisinglifelonglearners.com/executive-functioning-activities-for-small-children/

"15+ Executive Functioning Strategies Every Teacher Can Use." (2019). Pathway 2 Success. https://www.thepathway2success.com/15-executive-functioning-strategies-every-teacher-can-use/

"Cortex Matures Faster in Youth with Highest IQ." (2006). National Institutes of Health. https://www.nih.gov/news-events/news-releases/cortex-matures-faster-youth-highest-iq

Imposter Syndrome

Shoemaker, Jeffrey. (2014). "The Imposter Syndrome and Gifted Children." Ramblings of a Gifted Teacher. https://ramblingsofagiftedteacher.wordpress.com/2014/04/30/the-imposter-syndrome-and-gifted-children/

Ott, Tiffany. (2018). "I'm Just Not Smart Anymore – Imposter syndrome and Gifted Students." Teach Better. https://www.teachbetter.com/blog/imposter-syndrome-gifted-students/

Byrd, Ian. "The Curious Case of Imposter Syndrome." Byrdseed. https://www.byrdseed.com/the-curious-case-of-impostor-syndrome/

Kochis, Ginny. (2017). "Derailing Imposter Syndrome in Your Gifted Child." Not So Formulaic. https://notsoformulaic.com/1682-2

Sleep and the Gifted Child

Kessler, Colleen. (2018). "This is Why Your Gifted Child Struggles to Fall Asleep." Raising Lifelong Learners. https://raisinglifelonglearners.com/gifted-sleep-problems/

Kochis, Ginny. (2016). "No Rest for the Gifted (or Anxious or Sensitive): 5 Simple Tips to Encourage Restful Sleep." Not So Formulaic. https://notsoformulaic.com/no-rest-for-the-gifted-tips-for-bedtime-battles

Bainbridge, Carol. (2020). "Do Gifted Children Need Less Sleep?" VeryWell Family. https://www.verywellfamily.com/do-gifted-children-need-less-sleep-1448620

Bainbridge, Carol. (2020). "4 Tips to Help your Gifted Child Fall Asleep." VeryWell Family. https://www.verywellfamily.com/tips-to-help-your-gifted-child-fall-asleep-1449087

Index

2e 108, 109, 110, 111, 112, 117, 122, 151, 162, 163

A

AAEGT 65
academic ability 3, 6, 76, 77, 85, 86, 98
academic ability tests 98
academic placement 98
Accelerated/Honours high school/STEM residential high school 75
Acceleration 73, 75, 79, 81, 87, 148, 152, 160, 161
Acceleration in college 75, 79, 81
achievement tests 98
ADHD 31, 113, 115, 125, 148, 158, 164, 165
Advanced Placement 74, 84
age peer 71, 79, 86, 100
A Nation Deceived 73, 74, 75, 78, 160
A Nation Empowered 78, 161
anxiety 121, 126, 131, 132
ASD 113, 115, 148, 166
Susan Assouline 73, 86
asynchronous development 4, 5, 9, 10, 12, 14, 15, 68, 69, 72, 81, 135, 150
Attention Deficit Hyperactivity Disorder 113, 115, 148
Auditory Processing 45
Auditory Working Memory Index 31
Australian Association for the Education of the Gifted and Talented 65, 160
Autism Speaks 115
Autism Spectrum Disorder 113, 115, 148, 166
AWMI 31, 32

B

Belin-Blank Center 73, 86, 87, 152
Bell curve 52, 149
George Betts 119
Alfred Binet 22, 157
boredom 76, 77, 92, 112, 120

C

challenge 5, 5, 9, 62, 66, 68, 71, 76, 85, 91, 92, 116, 120, 135, 140, 145
cognitive 3, 4, 8, 10, 17, 19, 31, 37, 40, 42, 44, 45, 47, 48, 70, 98, 148, 149, 150, 159
Cognitive Proficiency Index 31, 37
Nicholas Colangelo 73
Columbus Group 4, 5
Combined classes 74
Comprehension Knowledge 44
Concurrent/dual enrolment 74, 79, 80
Continuous progress 74, 79
CPI 31, 37
Credit by examination 75
Curriculum compacting 74

D

Kazimierz Dąbrowski 123
Davidson Institute 55, 152, 156, 159
Davidson Young Scholars 64, 159
differentiation 71, 72, 76
Distance learning courses 74
dyscalculia 113, 164
dysgraphia 112, 113, 114, 163, 164
dyslexia 112, 113, 114, 163, 164
Dyspraxia 113, 115, 149, 165

E

Early admission to first grade 74
Early admission to kindergarten 74
Early entrance into middle school, high school or college 75
Early graduation from high school or college 75
educational consultants 5, 98
emotional 68, 69, 85, 87, 94, 96, 97, 99, 126, 148, 161, 169
emotional OE 126
energy 11, 91, 92, 93, 120, 125, 127, 128, 141
Exceptionally gifted 56
Executive function 135, 137
Extended Battery 44, 45, 47
Extension 78, 81

Extracurricular programmes 74, 79, 80

F

Facebook groups 63, 64
failure 76, 89, 119, 120, 122, 133
fantasies 126
fidget 125, 127
fine motor control 100, 114
fluid reasoning 19, 30, 44, 46, 47
Fluid Reasoning 24, 29, 36, 44
Fluid Reasoning Index 29, 36
Flynn Effect 19, 20, 26, 33, 156
FRI 29, 36
friendship 160
FSIQ 19, 24, 25, 28, 30, 31, 32, 35, 37, 38, 41, 44, 48, 49, 76, 97, 149
Full Scale IQ 149

G

Françoys Gagné 6, 7, 9, 11, 53, 149, 154
Gagné's Differentiated Model of Giftedness and Talent 6, 149, 154
GAI 31, 36, 37, 38, 49
GATE programmes 82, 83
General Ability Index 31, 36, 37, 44
GfGc 44
Gf/Gc Composite 44
Gifted Children South Africa 66, 160
Gifted Personality 118
gifted schools 83
goals 121, 122, 134
Grade skipping 74, 85
grey matter 5, 6
Miraca Gross 73
Grouping 81

H

Highly gifted 56
Hoagie's Gifted 55
Home schooling 83
Hong Kong Academy for Gifted Education 65, 160
hyperactive 115

I

imaginational OE 126
Imposter syndrome 139, 170
impulsive 115
inattentive 115
inherited trait 16
Institute for Educational Advancement 90, 153
Integrated Acceleration System 87
intellectual OE 126
International Baccalaureate 74, 84
International High IQ Society 62
Iowa Acceleration Scale 87
IQ test 4, 14, 16, 17, 18, 22, 26, 27, 41, 49, 51, 52, 53, 56, 59, 64, 65, 84, 97, 98, 109, 139, 150

J

Mary Bonner Johnson 42

K

knowledge 4, 7, 11, 37, 39, 41, 44, 46, 59, 61, 63, 67, 71, 89, 92, 101, 126, 129, 141, 146, 149

L

learning disability 110
Terman 22
Long-term Retrieval 45

M

MEG 5
melatonin 143
Mensa 5, 7, 49, 53, 62, 63, 64
Mentoring 74, 79, 80
Metacognition 126
Moderately gifted 56
MRI 5, 135

INDEX

N

NAGC 152, 153, 154, 155, 162, 163, 169
National Association for Gifted Children 7, 11, 152, 153, 154, 155, 163, 169
National Institute of Mental Health 135
National Research Center on the Gifted and Talented 8
Maureen Neihart 119
neural connections 6
neurological studies 5
neurotypical 5, 6, 10, 59, 61, 69, 70, 71, 75, 76, 77, 80, 85, 89, 100, 109, 116, 124, 135, 136, 139, 141, 145, 147
New Zealand Association for Gifted Children 65
Non-verbal Index 31, 36
Number Facility 45
NVI 31, 36

O

OE behaviour 127
overexcitabilities 123, 168

P

partial acceleration 74, 79
passion projects 120, 123, 129
Perceptual Speed 45
Perfectionism 133, 168, 169
Potential Plus UK 64
prefrontal cortex 135
Processing Speed 30, 36, 45
Profiles of the gifted and talented 119
profoundly gifted 72, 79, 92, 100
PSI 30, 31, 36
psychologist 1, 6, 8, 18, 22, 26, 71, 73, 74, 92, 95, 97, 109, 119, 123, 157
psychomotor OE 125

Q

QRI 31, 32
Quantitative Reasoning 24, 31
Quantitative Reasoning Index 31

R

rarity 53, 54, 55, 92
re-norming 20
Joseph Renzulli 8, 9, 75, 150, 154, 155
Deborah Ruf 56
Ruf's Levels of Giftedness 55, 59, 69, 159

S

SB-V 22, 23, 24, 25, 26, 33, 42
schooling 2, 9, 20, 62, 70, 72, 83, 146
Schooling methods 84
Self-paced instruction 74, 79
Sensory Processing Disorder 113, 116, 150, 166
sensual OE 125
Short-term Working Memory 44
Simon-Binet Intelligence Scale 22, 157
Sleep 140, 170, 171
social 16, 41, 63, 68, 69, 83, 85, 87, 99, 115, 124, 148, 161, 169
social and emotional maturity 99
social and emotional readiness 85
SPD 113, 116, 143, 150, 166
Standard Battery 44, 45
Standard deviation 150
Stanford-Binet 19, 21, 22, 23, 25, 27, 157
SB-V 22, 23, 24, 25, 26, 33, 42
Subject matter acceleration 74, 79
subtests 19, 24, 25, 27, 28, 29, 30, 31, 32, 33, 34, 35, 36, 37, 38, 39, 40, 41, 44, 45, 46, 47, 109, 157
support groups 2, 62, 71, 83, 117, 145

T

teachers 65, 67, 76, 77, 89, 93, 100, 102, 103, 106, 107, 111, 116, 119, 121, 123, 128, 132, 137, 146, 168
Telescoping curriculum 74, 79, 80
Theory of Positive Disintegration 123, 124, 167, 168
Three Ring Concept of Giftedness 8, 75
Stephanie Tolan 90
traits 5, 11, 59, 62, 118, 123, 144, 155
Twice-Exceptional 63, 108, 162, 163

V

VAI 36
VCI 29, 36
Verbal Comprehension Index 29, 36
Visual Processing 45
visual-spatial 32, 38, 39
Visual Spatial Index 29, 36
Vocabulary Acquisition Index 36
VSI 29, 36

W

WAIS 26, 28, 33, 34
Weschler Adult Intelligence Scale 26
Weschler-Bellevue Scale 26
David Weschler 26, 34
Weschler Intelligence Scale for Children 19, 21, 157
WISC 26, 27, 28, 30, 31, 32, 33, 34, 35, 42, 49, 157
Weschler Preschool and Primary Scale of Intelligence 19, 21, 34
WPPSI 19, 21, 34
WISC 26, 27, 28, 30, 31, 32, 33, 34, 35, 42, 49, 157
WMI 30, 31, 36, 37
Woodcock Johnson 19, 21, 42, 43, 158
Woodcock Johnson Test of Achievement 43
Woodcock Johnson Test of Cognitive Ability 42
Woodcock Johnson Test of Oral Language 42
Richard Woodcock 42
Working Memory 25, 30, 31, 36, 38, 44
Working Memory Index 30, 31, 36, 38
WPPSI 28, 33, 34, 35, 37, 41, 42, 49, 157, 158

www.ingramcontent.com/pod-product-compliance
Lightning Source LLC
Chambersburg PA
CBHW070559010526
44118CB00012B/1382